Wit Without Money by John Fletcher

A COMEDY

John Fletcher was born in December, 1579 in Rye, Sussex. He was baptised on December 20th.

As can be imagined details of much of his life and career have not survived and, accordingly, only a very brief indication of his life and works can be given.

Young Fletcher appears at the very young age of eleven to have entered Corpus Christi College at Cambridge University in 1591. There are no records that he ever took a degree but there is some small evidence that he was being prepared for a career in the church.

However what is clear is that this was soon abandoned as he joined the stream of people who would leave University and decamp to the more bohemian life of commercial theatre in London.

The upbringing of the now teenage Fletcher and his seven siblings now passed to his paternal uncle, the poet and minor official Giles Fletcher. Giles, who had the patronage of the Earl of Essex may have been a liability rather than an advantage to the young Fletcher. With Essex involved in the failed rebellion against Elizabeth Giles was also tainted.

By 1606 John Fletcher appears to have equipped himself with the talents to become a playwright. Initially this appears to have been for the Children of the Queen's Revels, then performing at the Blackfriars Theatre.

Fletcher's early career was marked by one significant failure; The Faithful Shepherdess, his adaptation of Giovanni Battista Guarini's Il Pastor Fido, which was performed by the Blackfriars Children in 1608.

By 1609, however, he had found his stride. With his collaborator John Beaumont, he wrote Philaster, which became a hit for the King's Men and began a profitable association between Fletcher and that company. Philaster appears also to have begun a trend for tragicomedy.

By the middle of the 1610s, Fletcher's plays had achieved a popularity that rivalled Shakespeare's and cemented the pre-eminence of the King's Men in Jacobean London. After his frequent early collaborator John Beaumont's early death in 1616, Fletcher continued working, both singly and in collaboration, until his own death in 1625. By that time, he had produced, or had been credited with, close to fifty plays.

Index of Contents

DRAMATIS PERSONAE
Valentine, a Gallant that will not be perswaded to keep his Estate.
Francisco, his younger Brother.
Master Lovegood their Uncle.
A Merchant, Friend to Master Lovegood.
Fountain   }
Bellamore   } companions of Valentine, and Sutors to the Widow.
Hairbrain   }
Lance, a Falkner, and an ancient servant to Valentines Father.
Shorthose, the Clown, and servant to the Widow.
Roger, Ralph, and Humphrey, three servants to the Widow.
Three Servants.
Musicians.
Lady Hartwel, a Widow.
Isabel, her Sister.
Luce, a waiting Gentlewoman to the Widow.

ACTUS PRIMUS

SCÆNA PRIMA

Enter **UNCLE** and **MERCHANT**.

MERCHANT
When saw you Valentine?

UNCLE
Not since the Horse-race, he's taken up with those that woo the Widow.

MERCHANT
How can he live by snatches from such people? he bore a worthy mind.

UNCLE
Alas, he's sunk, his means are gone, he wants, and which is worse,
Takes a delight in doing so.

MERCHANT

That's strange.

UNCLE
Runs Lunatick, if you but talk of states, he cannot be brought (now he has spent his own) to think there's inheritance, or means, but all a common riches, all men bound to be his Bailiffs.

MERCHANT
This is something dangerous.

UNCLE
No Gentleman that has estate to use it in keeping house, or followers, for those wayes he cries against, for Eating sins, dull Surfeits, cramming of Serving-men, mustering of Beggars, maintaining Hospitals for Kites, and Curs, grounding their fat faiths upon old Country proverbs, God bless the Founders; these he would have ventured into more manly uses, Wit, and carriage, and never thinks of state, or means, the ground-works: holding it monstrous, men should feed their bodies, and starve their understandings.

MERCHANT
That's most certain.

UNCLE
Yes, if he could stay there.

MERCHANT
Why let him marry, and that way rise again.

UNCLE
It's most impossible, he will not look with any handsomeness upon a Woman.

MERCHANT
Is he so strange to Women?

UNCLE
I know not what it is, a foolish glory he has got, I know not where, to balk those benefits, and yet he will converse and flatter 'em, make 'em, or fair, or foul, rugged, or smooth, as his impression serves, for he affirms, they are only lumps, and undigested pieces, lickt over to a form by our affections, and then they show. The Lovers let 'em pass.

[Enter **FOUNTAIN, BELLAMORE, HAIRBRIAN.**

MERCHANT
He might be one, he carries as much promise; they are wondrous merry.

UNCLE
O their hopes are high, Sir.

FOUNTAIN
Is Valentine come to Town?

BELLAMORE
Last night, I heard.

FOUNTAIN
We miss him monstrously in our directions, for this Widow is as stately, and as crafty, and stands I warrant you—

HAIRBRAIN
Let her stand sure, she falls before us else, come let's go seek Valentine.

MERCHANT
This Widow seems a Gallant.

UNCLE
A goodly Woman, and to her handsomness she bears her state, reserved, and great Fortune has made her Mistress of a full means, and well she knows to use it.

MERCHANT
I would Valentine had her.

UNCLE
There's no hope of that, Sir.

MERCHANT
O' that condition, he had his Mortgage in again.

UNCLE
I would he had.

MERCHANT
Seek means, and see what I'le do, however let the Money be paid in, I never sought a Gentlemans undoing, nor eat the bread of other mens vexations, you told me of another Brother.

UNCLE
Yes Sir, more miserable than he, for he has eat him, and drunk him up, a handsome Gentleman, and fine Scholar.

[Enter three **TENANTS**.

MERCHANT
What are these?

UNCLE
The Tenants, they'll do what they can.

MERCHANT
It is well prepared, be earnest, honest friends, and loud upon him, he is deaf to his own good.

LANCE
We mean to tell him part of our minds an't please you.

MERCHANT
Do, and do it home, and in what my care may help, or my perswasions when we meet next.

UNCLE
Do but perswade him fairly; and for your money, mine, and these mens thanks too, and what we can be able.

MERCHANT
Y'are most honest, you shall find me no less, and so I leave you, prosper your business my friends.

[Exit **MERCHANT**.

UNCLE
Pray Heaven it may, Sir.

LANCE
Nay if he will be mad, I'le be mad with him, and tell him that I'le not spare him, his Father kept good Meat, good Drink, good Fellows, good Hawks, good Hounds, and bid his Neighbours welcome; kept him too, and supplied his prodigality, yet kept his state still; must we turn Tenants now, after we have lived under the race of Gentry, and maintained good Yeomantry, to some of the City, to a great shoulder of Mutton and a Custard, and have our state turned into Cabbidge Gardens, must it be so?

UNCLE
You must be milder to him.

LANCE
That's as he makes his game.

UNCLE
Intreat him lovingly, and make him feel.

LANCE
I'le pinch him to the bones else.

VALENTINE [Within]
And tell the Gentleman, I'le be with him presently, say I want money too, I must not fail boy.

LANCE
You'l want Cloaths, I hope.

[Enter **VALENTINE**.

VALENTINE
Bid the young Courtier repair to me anon, I'le read to him.

UNCLE

He comes, be diligent, but not too rugged, start him, but affright him not.

VALENTINE

Phew, are you there?

UNCLE

We come to see you Nephew, be not angry.

VALENTINE

Why do you dog me thus, with these strange people? why, all the world shall never make me rich more, nor master of these troubles.

TENANTS

We beseech you for our poor Childrens sake.

VALENTINE

Who bid you get 'em? have you not threshing work enough, but Children must be bang'd out o'th' sheaf too? other men with all their delicates, and healthful diets, can get but wind eggs: you with a clove of Garlick, a piece of Cheese would break a Saw, and sowre Milk, can mount like Stallions, and I must maintain these tumblers.

LANCE

You ought to maintain us, we have maintained you, and when you slept provided for you; who bought the Silk you wear? I think our labours; reckon, you'll find it so: who found your Horses perpetual pots of Ale, maintain'd your Taverns, and who extol'd you in the Half-crown-boxes, where you might sit and muster all the Beauties? we had no hand in these; no, we are all puppies? Your Tenants base vexations.

VALENTINE

Very well, Sir.

LANCE

Had you Land, Sir, and honest men to serve your purposes, honest and faithful, and will you run away from 'em, betray your self, and your poor Tribe to misery; mortgage all us, like old Cloaks; where will you hunt next? you had a thousand Acres, fair and open: The Kings-Bench is enclos'd, there's no good riding, the Counter is full of thorns and brakes, take heed Sir, and boggs, you'l quickly find what broth they're made of.

VALENTINE

Y'are short and pithy.

LANCE

They say y'are a fine Gentleman, and of excellent judgement, they report you have a wit; keep your self out o'th' Rain, and take your Cloak with you, which by interpretation is your State, Sir, or I shall think your fame belied you, you have money, and may have means.

VALENTINE

I prethee leave prating, does my good lye within thy brain to further, or my undoing in thy pity? go, go, get you home, there whistle to your Horses, and let them edifie; away, sow Hemp to hang your selves withal: what am I to you, or you to me; am I your Landlord, puppies?

UNCLE
This is uncivil.

VALENTINE
More unmerciful you, to vex me with these Bacon Broth and Puddings, they are the walking shapes of all my sorrows.

3 TENANTS
Your Fathers Worship would have used us better.

VALENTINE
My Fathers Worship was a Fool.

LANCE
Hey, hey boys, old Valentine i'faith, the old boy still.

UNCLE
Fie Cousin.

VALENTINE
I mean besotted to his state, he had never left me the misery of so much means else, which till I sold, was a meer meagrim to me: If you will talk, turn out these Tenants, they are as killing to my nature Uncle, as water to a Feaver.

LANCE
We will go, but it is like Rams, to come again the stronger, and you shall keep your state.

VALENTINE
Thou lyest, I will not.

LANCE
Sweet Sir, thou lyest, thou shalt, and so good morrow.

[Exeunt **TENANTS**.

VALENTINE
This was my man, and of a noble breeding: now to your business Uncle.

UNCLE
To your state then.

VALENTINE
'Tis gone, and I am glad on't, name it no more, 'tis that I pray against, and Heaven has heard me, I tell you, Sir, I am more fearful of it, I mean, of thinking of more lands, or livings, than sickly men are

travelling o' Sundays, for being quell'd with Carriers; out upon't, caveat emptor, let the fool out-sweat it, that thinks he has got a catch on't.

UNCLE
This is madness to be a wilful begger.

VALENTINE
I am mad then, and so I mean to be, will that content you? How bravely now I live, how jocund, how near the first inheritance, without fears, how free from title-troubles!

UNCLE
And from means too.

VALENTINE
Means? why all good men's my means; my wit's my Plow, the Town's my stock, Tavern's my standing-house, and all the world knows there's no want; all Gentlemen that love Society, love me; all Purses that wit and pleasure opens, are my Tenants; every mans Cloaths fit me, the next fair lodging is but my next remove, and when I please to be more eminent, and take the Air, a piece is levied, and a Coach prepared, and I go I care not whither, what need state here?

UNCLE
But say these means were honest, will they last, Sir?

VALENTINE
Far longer than your jerkin, and wear fairer, should I take ought of you, 'tis true, I beg'd now, or which is worse than that, I stole a kindness, and which is worst of all, I lost my way in't; your mind's enclosed, nothing lies open nobly, your very thoughts are Hinds that work on nothing but daily sweat and trouble: were my way so full of dirt as this, 'tis true I'd shift it; are my acquaintance Grasiers? but Sir, know, no man that I am allied to, in my living, but makes it equal, whether his own use, or my necessity pull first, nor is this forc'd, but the meer quality and poisure of goodness, and do you think I venture nothing equal?

UNCLE
You pose me Cousin.

VALENTINE
What's my knowledge Uncle, is't not worth mony? what's my understanding, travel, reading, wit, all these digested, my daily making men, some to speak, that too much flegm had frozen up, some that spoke too much, to hold their peace, and put their tongues to pensions, some to wear their cloaths, and some to keep 'em, these are nothing Uncle; besides these wayes, to teach the way of nature, a manly love, community to all that are deservers, not examining how much, or what's done for them, 'tis wicked, and such a one like you, chews his thoughts double, making 'em only food for his repentance.

[Enter two **SERVANTS**.

1ˢᵀ SERVANT
This cloak and hat Sir, and my Masters love.

VALENTINE

Commend's to thy Master, and take that, and leave 'em at my
lodging.

1ST SERVANT

I shall do it Sir.

VALENTINE

I do not think of these things.

2ND SERVANT

Please you Sir, I have gold here for you.

VALENTINE

Give it me, drink that and commend me to thy Master; look you Uncle, do I beg these?

UNCLE

No sure, 'tis your worth, Sir.

VALENTINE

'Tis like enough, but pray satisfie me, are not these ways as honest as persecuting the starved
inheritance, with musty Corn, the very rats were fain to run away from, or felling rotten wood by the
pound, like spices, which Gentlemen do after burn by th' ounces? do not I know your way of feeding
beasts with grains, and windy stuff, to blow up Butchers? your racking Pastures, that have eaten up as
many singing Shepherds, and their issues, as Andeluzia breeds? these are authentique, I tell you Sir, I
would not change ways with you, unless it were to sell your state that hour, and if it were possible to
spend it then too, for all your Beans in Rumnillo, now you know me.

UNCLE

I would you knew your self, but since you are grown such a strange enemy to all that fits you, give me
leave to make your Brothers fortune.

VALENTINE

How?

UNCLE

From your mortgage, which yet you may recover, I'le find the means.

VALENTINE

Pray save your labour Sir, my Brother and my self will run one fortune, and I think what I hold a meer
vexation, cannot be safe for him, I love him better, he has wit at will, the world has means, he shall live
without this trick of state, we are heirs both, and all the world before us.

UNCLE

My last offer, and then I am gone.

VALENTINE

What is't, and then I'le answer.

UNCLE
What think you of a wife yet to restore you, and tell me seriously without these trifles.

VALENTINE
And you can find one, that can please my fancy, you shall not find me stubborn.

UNCLE
Speak your Woman.

VALENTINE
One without eyes, that is, self commendations, for when they find they are handsom, they are unwholsome; one without ears, not giving time to flatterers, for she that hears her self commended, wavers, and points men out a way to make 'em wicked; one without substance of her self; that woman without the pleasure of her life, that's wanton; though she be young, forgetting it, though fair, making her glass the eyes of honest men, not her own admiration, all her ends obedience, all her hours new blessings, if there may be such a woman.

UNCLE
Yes there may be.

VALENTINE
And without state too.

UNCLE
You are disposed to trifle, well, fare you well Sir, when you want me next, you'l seek me out a better sence.

VALENTINE
Farewell Uncle, and as you love your estate, let not me hear on't.

[Exit.

UNCLE
It shall not trouble you, I'le watch him still,
And when his friends fall off then bend his will.

[Exit.

[Enter **ISABELLA** and **LUCE**.

LUCE
I know the cause of all this sadness now, your sister has ingrost all the brave Lovers.

ISABELLA
She has wherewithall, much good may't do her, prethee speak softly, we are open to mens ears.

LUCE

Fear not, we are safe, we may see all that pass, hear all, and make our selves merry with their language, and yet stand undiscovered, be not melancholy, you are as fair as she.

ISABELLA
Who I? I thank you, I am as haste ordain'd me, a thing slubber'd, my sister is a goodly portly Lady, a woman of a presence, she spreads sattens, as the Kings ships do canvas every where, she may spare me her misen, and her bonnets, strike her main Petticoat, and yet outsail me, I am a Carvel to her.

LUCE
But a tight one.

ISABELLA
She is excellent, well built too.

LUCE
And yet she's old.

ISABELLA
She never saw above one voyage Luce, and credit me after another, her Hull will serve again, a right good Merchant: she plaies, and sings too, dances and discourses, comes very near Essays, a pretty Poet, begins to piddle with Philosophic, a subtil Chymick Wench, and can extract the Spirit of mens Estates, she has the light before her, and cannot miss her choice for me, 'tis reason I wait my mean fortune.

LUCE
You are so bashfull.

ISABELLA
It is not at first word up and ride, thou art cozen'd, that would shew mad i' faith: besides, we lose the main part of our politick government: if we become provokers, then we are fair, and fit for mens imbraces, when like towns, they lie before us ages, yet not carried, hold out their strongest batteries, then compound too without the loss of honour, and march off with our fair wedding, Colours flying. Who are these?

[Enter **FRANCISCO** and **LANCE**.

LUCE
I know not, nor I care not.

ISABELLA
Prethee peace then, a well built Gentleman.

LUCE
But poorly thatcht.

LANCE
Has he devour'd you too?

FRANCISCO

H'as gulp'd me down Lance.

LANCE
Left you no means to study?

FRANCISCO
Not a farthing: dispatcht my poor annuity I thank him, here's all the hope I have left, one bare ten shillings.

LANCE
You are fit for great mens services.

FRANCISCO
I am fit, but who'le take me thus? mens miseries are now accounted stains in their natures. I have travelled, and I have studied long, observed all Kingdoms, know all the promises of Art and manners, yet that I am not bold, nor cannot flatter, I shall not thrive, all these are but vain Studies, art thou so rich as to get me a lodging Lance?

LANCE
I'le sell the titles of my house else, my Horse, my Hawk, nay's death I'le pawn my wife: Oh Mr. Francis, that I should see your Fathers house fall thus!

ISABELLA
An honest fellow.

LANCE
Your Fathers house, that fed me, that bred up all my name!

ISABELLA
A gratefull fellow.

LANCE
And fall by—

FRANCISCO
Peace, I know you are angry Lance, but I must not hear with whom, he is my Brother, and though you hold him slight, my most dear Brother: A Gentleman, excepting some few rubs, he were too excellent to live here else, fraughted as deep with noble and brave parts, the issues of a noble and manly Spirit, as any he alive. I must not hear you; though I am miserable, and he made me so, yet still he is my Brother, still I love him, and to that tye of blood link my affections.

ISABELLA
A noble nature! dost thou know him Luce?

LUCE
No, Mistress.

ISABELLA

Thou shouldest ever know such good men, what a fair body and mind are married! did he not say he wanted?

LUCE
What's that to you?

ISABELLA
'Tis true, but 'tis great pity.

LUCE
How she changes! ten thousand more than he, as handsom men too.

ISABELLA
'Tis like enough, but as I live, this Gentleman among ten thousand thousand! is there no knowing him? why should he want? fellows of no merit, slight and puft souls, that walk like shadows, by leaving no print of what they are, or poise, let them complain.

LUCE
Her colour changes strangely.

ISABELLA
This man was made, to mark his wants to waken us; alas poor Gentleman, but will that keep him from cold and hunger, believe me he is well bred, and cannot be but of a noble linage, mark him, mark him well.

LUCE
'Is a handsom man.

ISABELLA
The sweetness of his sufferance sets him off, O Luce, but whither go I?

LUCE
You cannot hide it.

ISABELLA
I would he had what I can spare.

LUCE
'Tis charitable.

LANCE
Come Sir, I'le see you lodg'd, you have tied my tongue fast, I'le steal before you want, 'tis but a hanging.

ISABELLA
That's a good fellow too, an honest fellow, why, this would move a stone, I must needs know; but that some other time.

[Exit **LANCE** and **FRANCISCO**.

LUCE
Is the wind there? that makes for me.

ISABELLA
Come, I forgot a business.

ACTUS SECUNDUS

SCÆNA PRIMA

Enter **WIDOW** and **LUCE**.

WIDOW
My sister, and a woman of so base a pity! what was the fellow?

LUCE
Why, an ordinary man, Madam.

WIDOW
Poor?

LUCE
Poor enough, and no man knows from whence neither.

WIDOW
What could she see?

LUCE
Only his misery, for else she might behold a hundred handsomer.

WIDOW
Did she change much?

LUCE
Extreamly, when he spoke, and then her pity, like an Orator, I fear her love framed such a commendation, and followed it so far, as made me wonder.

WIDOW
Is she so hot, or such a want of lovers, that she must doat upon afflictions? why does she not go romage all the prisons, and there bestow her youth, bewray her wantonness, and flie her honour, common both to beggery: did she speak to him?

LUCE
No, he saw us not, but ever since, she hath been mainly troubled.

WIDOW
Was he young?

LUCE
Yes, young enough.

WIDOW
And looked he like a Gentleman?

LUCE
Like such a Gentleman, that would pawn ten oaths for twelve pence.

WIDOW
My sister, and sink basely! this must not be, does she use means to know him?

LUCE
Yes Madam, and has employed a Squire called Shorthose.

WIDOW
O that's a precious Knave: keep all this private, but still be near her lodging: Luce, what you can gather by any means, let me understand: I'le stop her heat, and turn her charity another way, to bless her self first; be still close to her counsels; a begger and a stranger! there's a bless'dness! I'le none of that; I have a toy yet, sister, shall tell you this is foul, and make you find it, and for your pains take you the last gown I wore; this makes me mad, but I shall force a remedy.

[Enter **FOUNTAIN, BELLAMORE, HAIRBRAIN, VALENTINE.**

FOUNTAIN
Sirra, we have so lookt for thee, and long'd for thee; this widow is the strangest thing, the stateliest, and stands so much upon her excellencies.

BELLAMORE
She hath put us off, this month now, for an answer.

HAIRBRAIN
No man must visit her, nor look upon her, no, not say, good morrow, nor good even, till that's past.

VALENTINE
She has found what dough you are made of, and so kneads you: are you good at nothing, but these after-games? I have told you often enough what things they are, what precious things, these widows—

HAIRBRAIN
If we had 'em.

VALENTINE
Why the Devil has not craft enough to wooe 'em, there be three kinds of fools, mark this note Gentlemen, mark it, and understand it.

FOUNTAIN
Well, go forward.

VALENTINE
An Innocent, a knave fool, a fool politick: the last of which are lovers, widow lovers.

BELLAMORE
Will you allow no fortune?

VALENTINE
No such blind one.

FOUNTAIN
We gave you reasons, why 'twas needful for us.

VALENTINE
As you are those fools, I did allow those reasons, but as my Scholars and companions damn'd 'em: do you know what it is to wooe a widow? answer me coolely now, and understandingly.

HAIRBRAIN
Why to lie with her, and to enjoy her wealth.

VALENTINE
Why there you are fools still, crafty to catch your selves, pure politick fools, I lookt for such an answer; once more hear me, it is, to wed a widow, to be doubted mainly, whether the state you have be yours or no, or those old boots you ride in. Mark me, widows are long extents in Law upon news, livings upon their bodies winding-sheets, they that enjoy 'em, lie but with dead mens monuments, and beget only their own ill Epitaphs: Is not this plain now?

BELLAMORE
Plain spoken.

VALENTINE
And plain truth; but if you'le needs do things of danger, do but lose your selves, not any part concerns your understandings, for then you are Meacocks, fools, and miserable march off amain, within an inch of a Fircug, turn me o'th' toe like a Weather-cock, kill every day a Sergeant for a twelve month, rob the Exchequer, and burn all the Rolls, and these will make a shew.

HAIRBRAIN
And these are trifles.

VALENTINE
Considered to a Widow, empty nothings, for here you venture but your persons, there the varnish of your persons, your discretions; why 'tis a monstrous thing to marry at all, especially as now 'tis made; me thinks a man, an understanding man, is more wise to me, and of a nobler tie, than all these trinkets; what do we get by women, but our senses, which is the rankest part about us, satisfied, and when that's done, what are we? Crest-fallen Cowards. What benefit can children be, but charges and disobedience? What's the love they render at one and twenty years? I pray die Father: when they are young, they are

like bells rung backwards, nothing but noise and giddiness; and come to years once, there drops a son by th' sword in his Mistresses quarrel, a great joy to his parents: A Daughter ripe too, grows high and lusty in her blood, must have a heating, runs away with a supple ham'd Servingman: his twenty Nobles spent, takes to a trade, and learns to spin mens hair off; there's another, and most are of this nature, will you marry?

FOUNTAIN
For my part yes, for any doubt I feel yet.

VALENTINE
And this same widow?

FOUNTAIN
If I may, and me thinks, however you are pleased to dispute these dangers, such a warm match, and for you, Sir, were not hurtfull.

VALENTINE
Not half so killing as for you, for me she cannot with all the Art she has, make me more miserable, or much more fortunate, I have no state left, a benefit that none of you can brag of, and there's the Antidote against a Widow, nothing to lose, but that my soul inherits, which she can neither law nor claw away; to that, but little flesh, it were too much else; and that unwholsom too, it were too rich else; and to all this contempt of what she do's I can laugh at her tears, neglect her angers, hear her without a faith, so pity her as if she were a Traytour, moan her person, but deadly hate her pride; if you could do these, and had but this discretion, and like fortune, it were but an equal venture.

FOUNTAIN
This is malice.

VALENTINE
When she lies with your land, and not with you, grows great with joyntures, and is brought to bed with all the state you have, you'le find this certain; but is it come to pass you must marry, is there no buff will hold you?

BELLAMORE
Grant it be so.

VALENTINE
Then chuse the tamer evil, take a maid, a maid not worth a penny; make her yours, knead her, and mould her yours, a maid worth nothing, there's a vertuous spell in that word nothing; a maid makes conscience of half a Crown a week for pins and puppits, a maid will be content with one Coach and two Horses, not falling out because they are not matches; with one man satisfied, with one rein guided, with one faith, one content, one bed, aged she makes the wise, preserves the fame and issue; a widow is a Christmas-box that sweeps all.

FOUNTAIN
Yet all this cannot sink us.

VALENTINE

You are my friends, and all my loving friends, I spend your mony, yet I deserve it too, you are my friends still, I ride your horses, when I want I sell 'em; I eat your meat, help to wear her linnen, sometimes I make you drunk, and then you seal, for which I'le do you this commodity, be ruled, and let me try her, I will discover her, the truth is, I will never leave to trouble her, till I see through her, then if I find her worthy.

HAIRBRAIN
This was our meaning Valentine.

VALENTINE
'Tis done then, I must want nothing.

HAIRBRAIN
Nothing but the woman.

VALENTINE
No jealousie; for when I marry, the Devil must be wiser than I take him; and the flesh foolisher: come let's to dinner, and when I am well whetted with wine, have at her.

[Exeunt.

[Enter **ISABELLA** and **LUCE**.

ISABELLA
But art thou sure?

LUCE
No surer than I heard.

HAIRBRAIN
That it was that flouting fellows Brother?

LUCE
Yes, Shorthose told me so.

HAIRBRAIN
He did search out the truth?

LUCE
It seems he did.

HAIRBRAIN
Prethee Luce call him hither, if he be no worse, I never repent my pity, now sirra, what was he we sent you after, the Gentleman i'th' black?

[Enter **SHORTHOSE**.

SHORTHOSE

I'th' torn black?

ISABELLA
Yes, the same Sir.

SHORTHOSE
What would your Worship with him?

ISABELLA
Why, my Worship would know his name, and what he is.

SHORTHOSE
'Is nothing, he is a man, and yet he is no man.

ISABELLA
You must needs play the fool.

SHORTHOSE
'Tis my profession.

ISABELLA
How is he a man, and no man?

SHORTHOSE
He's a begger, only the sign of a man, the bush pull'd down, which shows the house stands emptie.

ISABELLA
What's his calling?

SHORTHOSE
They call him begger.

ISABELLA
What's his kindred?

SHORTHOSE
Beggers.

ISABELLA
His worth?

SHORTHOSE
A learned begger, a poor Scholar.

ISABELLA
How does he live?

SHORTHOSE

Like worms, he eats old Books.

ISABELLA
Is Valentine his Brother.

SHORTHOSE
His begging Brother.

ISABELLA
What may his name be?

SHORTHOSE
Orson.

ISABELLA
Leave your fooling.

SHORTHOSE
You had as good say, leave your living.

ISABELLA
Once more tell me his name directly.

SHORTHOSE
I'le be hang'd first, unless I heard him Christned, but I can tell what foolish people call him.

ISABELLA
What?

SHORTHOSE
Francisco.

ISABELLA
Where lies this learning, Sir?

SHORTHOSE
In Pauls Church yard forsooth.

ISABELLA
I mean the Gentleman, fool.

SHORTHOSE
O that fool, he lies in loose sheets every where, that's no where.

LUCE
You have glean'd since you came to London: in the Country, Shorthose, you were an arrant fool, a dull cold coxcombe, here every Tavern teaches you, the pint pot has so belaboured you with wit, your brave acquaintance that gives you Ale, so fortified your mazard, that now there's no talking to you.

ISABELLA

'Is much improved, a fellow, a fine discourser.

SHORTHOSE

I hope so, I have not waited at the tail of wit so long to be an Ass.

LUCE

But say now, Shorthose, my Lady should remove into the Country.

SHORTHOSE

I had as lieve she should remove to Heaven, and as soon I would undertake to follow her.

LUCE

Where no old Charnico is, nor no Anchoves, nor Master such-a-one, to meet at the Rose, and bring my Lady, such-a-ones chief Chamber-maid.

ISABELLA

No bouncing healths to this brave Lad, dear Shorthose, nor down o'th' knees to that illustrious Lady.

LUCE

No fiddles, nor no lusty noise of drawer, carry this pottle to my Father Shorthose.

ISABELLA

No plays, nor gaily foists, no strange Embassadors to run and wonder at, till thou beest oyl, and then come home again, and lye byth' Legend.

LUCE

Say she should go.

SHORTHOSE

If I say, I'le be hang'd, or if I thought she would go.

LUCE

What?

SHORTHOSE

I would go with her.

LUCE

But Shorthose, where thy heart is?

ISABELLA

Do not fright him.

LUCE

By this hand Mistris 'tis a noise, a loud one too, and from her own mouth, presently to be gone too, but why, or to what end?

SHORTHOSE
May not a man die first? she'l give him so much time.

ISABELLA
Gone o'th' sudden? thou dost but jest, she must not mock the Gentlemen.

LUCE
She has put them off a month, they dare not see her, believe me Mistris, what I hear I tell you.

ISABELLA
Is this true, wench? gone on so short a warning! what trick is this? she never told me of it, it must not be, sirra, attend me presently, you know I have been a carefull friend unto you, attend me in the Hall, and next be faithful, cry not, we shall not go.

SHORTHOSE
Her Coach may crack.

[Enter **VALENTINE**, **FRANCISCO** and **LANCE**.

VALENTINE
Which way to live! how darest thou come to town, to ask such an idle question?

FRANCISCO
Me thinks 'tis necessary, unless you could restore that Annuitie you have tipled up in Taverns.

VALENTINE
Where hast thou been, and how brought up Francisco, that thou talkest thus out of France? thou wert a pretty fellow, and of a handsom knowledge; who has spoiled thee?

LANCE
He that has spoil'd himself, to make him sport, and by Copie, will spoil all comes near him: buy but a Glass, if you be yet so wealthy, and look there who?

VALENTINE
Well said, old Copihold.

LANCE
My heart's good Freehold Sir, and so you'l find it, this Gentleman's your Brother, your hopeful Brother, for there is no hope of you, use him thereafter.

VALENTINE
E'ne as well as I use my self, what would'st thou have Frank?

FRANCISCO
Can you procure me a hundred pound?

LANCE

Hark what he saies to you, O try your wits, they say you are excellent at it, for your Land has lain long bedrid, and unsensible.

FRANCISCO
And I'le forget all wrongs, you see my state, and to what wretchedness your will has brought me; but what it may be, by this benefit, if timely done, and like a noble Brother, both you and I may feel, and to our comforts.

VALENTINE
A hundred pound! dost thou know what thou hast said Boy?

FRANCISCO
I said a hundred pound.

VALENTINE
Thou hast said more than any man can justifie, believe it: procure a hundred pounds! I say to thee there's no such sum in nature, forty shillings there may be now i'th' Mint and that's a Treasure, I have seen five pound, but let me tell it, and 'tis as wonderful as Calves with five Legs; here's five shillings, Frank, the harvest of five weeks, and a good crop too, take it, and pay thy first fruits, I'le come down and eat it out.

FRANCISCO
'Tis patience must meet with you Sir, not love.

LANCE
Deal roundly, and leave these fiddle faddles.

VALENTINE
Leave thy prating, thou thinkest thou art a notable wise fellow, thou and thy rotten Sparrow Hawk; two of the reverent.

LANCE
I think you are mad, or if you be not, will be, with the next moon, what would you have him do?

VALENTINE
How?

LANCE
To get money first, that's to live, you have shewed him how to want.

VALENTINE
'Slife how do I live? why, what dull fool would ask that question? three hundred three pilds more, I and live bravely: the better half o'th' Town live most gloriously, and ask them what states they have, or what Annuities, or when they pray for seasonable Harvests: thou hast a handsome Wit, stir into the world, Frank, stir, stir for shame, thou art a pretty Scholar: ask how to live? write, write, write any thing, the World's a fine believing World, write News.

LANCE

Dragons in Sussex, Sir, or fiery Battels seen in the Air at Aspurge.

VALENTINE
There's the way Frank, and in the tail of these, fright me the Kingdom with a sharp Prognostication, that shall scowr them, Dearth upon Dearth, like leven Taffaties, predictions of Sea-breaches, Wars, and want of Herrings on our Coast, with bloudy Noses.

LANCE
Whirl-winds, that shall take off the top of Grantham Steeple, and clap it on Pauls, and after these, a Lenvoy to the City for their sins.

VALENTINE
Probatum est, thou canst not want a pension, go switch me up a Covey of young Scholars, there's twenty nobles, and two loads of Coals, are not these ready wayes? Cosmography thou art deeply read in, draw me a Map from the Mermaid, I mean a midnight Map to scape the Watches, and such long sensless examinations, and Gentlemen shall feed thee, right good Gentlemen, I cannot stay long.

LANCE
You have read learnedly, and would you have him follow these Megera's, did you begin with Ballads?

FRANCISCO
Well, I will leave you, I see my wants are grown ridiculous, yours may be so, I will not curse you neither; you may think, when these wanton fits are over, who bred me, and who ruined me, look to your self, Sir, a providence I wait on.

VALENTINE
Thou art passionate, hast thou been brought up with Girls?

[Enter **SHORTHOSE** with a bag.

SHORTHOSE
Rest you merry, Gentlemen.

VALENTINE
Not so merry as you suppose, Sir.

SHORTHOSE
Pray stay a while, and let me take a view of you, I may put my Spoon into the wrong Pottage-pot else.

VALENTINE
Why, wilt thou muster us?

SHORTHOSE
No, you are not he, you are a thought too handsome.

LANCE
Who wouldst thou speak withal, why dost thou peep so?

SHORTHOSE
I am looking birds nests, I can find none in your bush beard, I would speak with you, black Gentleman.

FRANCISCO
With me, my friend?

SHORTHOSE
Yes sure, and the best friend, Sir, it seems you spake withal this twelve-month, Gentleman, there's money for you.

VALENTINE
How?

SHORTHOSE
There's none for you, Sir, be not so brief, not a penny; law how he itches at it, stand off, you stir my colour.

LANCE
Take it, 'tis money.

SHORTHOSE
You are too quick too, first be sure you have it, you seem to be a Faulkoner, but a foolish one.

LANCE
Take it, and say nothing.

SHORTHOSE
You are cozen'd too, 'tis take it, and spend it.

FRANCISCO
From whom came it, Sir?

SHORTHOSE
Such another word, and you shall have none on't.

FRANCISCO
I thank you, Sir, I doubly thank you.

SHORTHOSE
Well, Sir, then buy you better Cloaths, and get your Hat drest, and your Laundress to wash your Boots white.

FRANCISCO
Pray stay Sir, may you not be mistaken.

SHORTHOSE
I think I am, give me the money again, come quick, quick, quick.

FRANCISCO
I would be loth to render, till I am sure it be so.

SHORTHOSE
Hark in your ear, is not your name Francisco?

FRANCISCO
Yes.

SHORTHOSE
Be quiet then, it may Thunder a hundred times, before such stones fall: do you not need it?

FRANCISCO
Yes.

SHORTHOSE
And 'tis thought you have it.

FRANCISCO
I think I have.

SHORTHOSE
Then hold it fast, 'tis not fly-blown, you may pay for the poundage, you forget your self, I have not seen a Gentleman so backward, a wanting Gentleman.

FRANCISCO
Your mercy, Sir.

SHORTHOSE
Friend, you have mercy, a whole bag full of mercy, be merry with it, and be wise.

FRANCISCO
I would fain, if it please you, but know—

SHORTHOSE
It does not please me, tell over your money, and be not mad, Boy.

VALENTINE
You have no more such bags?

SHORTHOSE
More such there are, Sir, but few I fear for you, I have cast your water, you have wit, you need no money.

[Exit.

LANCE

Be not amazed, Sir, 'tis good gold, good old gold, this is restorative, and in good time, it comes to do you good, keep it and use it, let honest fingers feel it, yours be too quick Sir.

FRANCISCO
He named me, and he gave it me, but from whom.

LANCE
Let 'em send more, and then examine it, this can be but a Preface.

FRANCISCO
Being a stranger, of whom can I deserve this?

LANCE
Sir, of any man that has but eyes, and manly understanding to find mens wants, good men are bound to do so.

VALENTINE
Now you see, Frank, there are more wayes than certainties, now you believe: What Plough brought you this Harvest, what sale of Timber, Coals, or what Annuities? These feed no Hinds, nor wait the expectation of Quarterdaies, you see it showers in to you, you are an Ass, lie plodding, and lie fooling, about this Blazing Star, and that bo-peep, whining, and fasting, to find the natural reason why a Dog turns twice about before he lie down, what use of these, or what joy in Annuities, where every man's thy study, and thy Tenant, I am ashamed on thee.

LANCE
Yes, I have seen this fellow, there's a wealthy Widow hard by.

VALENTINE
Yes marry is there.

LANCE
I think he's her servant, or I am couzen'd else, I am sure on't.

FRANCISCO
I am glad on't.

LANCE
She's a good Woman.

FRANCISCO
I am gladder.

LANCE
And young enough believe.

FRANCISCO
I am gladder of all, Sir.

VALENTINE
Francisoc, you shall lye with me soon.

FRANCISCO
I thank my money.

LANCE
His money shall lie with me, three in a Bed, Sir, will be too much this weather.

VALENTINE
Meet me at the Mermaid, and thou shalt see what things—

LANCE
Trust to your self Sir.

[Exeunt **FRANCISCO** and **VALENTINE**.

[Enter **FOUNTAIN**, **BELLAMORE** and **VALENTINE**.

FOUNTAIN
O Valentine!

VALENTINE
How now, why do you look so?

BELLAMORE
The Widow's going, man.

VALENTINE
Why let her go, man.

HAIRBRAIN
She's going out o'th' Town.

VALENTINE
The Town's the happier, I would they were all gone.

FOUNTAIN
We cannot come to speak with her.

VALENTINE
Not to speak to her?

BELLAMORE
She will be gone within this hour, either now Valentine.

FOUNTAIN & HAIRBRAIN
Now, now, now, good Valentine.

VALENTINE
I had rather march i'th' mouth o'th' Cannon, but adiew, if she be above ground, go, away to your prayers, away I say, away, she shall be spoken withall.

[Exeunt.

[Enter **SHORTHOSE** with one boot on, **ROGER** and **HUMPHREY**.

ROGER
She will go, Shorthose.

SHORTHOSE
Who can help it Roger?

RALPH [within]
Help down with the hangings.

ROGER
By and by Ralph
I am making up o'th' trunks here.

RALPH
Shorthose.

SHORTHOSE
Well.

RALPH
Who looks to my Ladys wardrobe? Humphrey.

HUMPHREY
Here.

RALPH
Down with the boxes in the gallery, and bring away the
Coach cushions.

SHORTHOSE
Will it not rain, no conjuring abroad, nor no devices to stop this journey?

ROGER
Why go now, why now, why o'th' sudden now? what preparation, what horses have we ready, what provision laid in i'th' Country?

HUMPHREY
Not an egge I hope.

ROGER
No nor one drop of good drink boyes, there's the devil.

SHORTHOSE
I heartily pray the malt be musty, and then we must come up again.

HUMPHREY
What sayes the Steward?

ROGER
He's at's wits end, for some four hours since, out of his haste and providence, he mistook the Millars mangie mare, for his own nagge.

SHORTHOSE
And she may break his neck, and save the journy. Oh London how I love thee!

HUMPHREY
I have no boots nor none I'le buy: or if I had, refuse me if I would venture my ability, before a Cloak-Bag, men are men.

SHORTHOSE
For my part, if I be brought, as I know it will be aimed at, to carry any durty dairy Cream-pot, or any gentle Lady of the Laundry, Chambring, or wantonness behind my Gelding, with all her Streamers, Knapsacks, Glasses, Gugawes, as if I were a running flippery, I'le give 'em leave to cut my girts, and slay me. I'le not be troubled with their Distibations, at every half miles end, I understand my self, and am resolved.

HUMPHREY
To morrow night at Olivers! who shall be there boys, who shall meet the wenches?

ROGER
The well brew'd stand of Ale, we should have met at!

SHORTHOSE
These griefs like to another Tale of Troy, would mollifie the hearts of barbarous people, and Tom Butcher weep, Aeneas enters, and now the town's lost.

RALPH
Well whither run you, my Lady is mad.

SHORTHOSE
I would she were in Bedlam.

RALPH
The carts are come, no hands to help to load 'em? the stuff lies in the hall, the plate.

WIDOW [within]
Why knaves there, where be these idle fellows?

SHORTHOSE
Shall I ride with one Boot?

WIDOW
Why where I say?

RALPH
Away, away, it must be so.

SHORTHOSE
O for a tickling storm, to last but ten days.

[Exeunt.

Enter **ISABELLA** and **LUCE**.

LUCE
By my troth Mistris I did it for the best.

ISABELLA
It may be so, but Luce, you have a tongue, a dish of meat in your mouth, which if it were minced Luce, would do a great deal better.

LUCE
I protest Mistress.

ISABELLA
It will be your own one time or other: Walter.

WALTER [within]
Anon forsooth.

ISABELLA
Lay my hat ready, my fan and cloak, you are so full of providence; and Walter, tuck up my little box behind the Coach, and bid my maid make ready, my sweet service to your good Lady Mistress; and my dog, good let the Coachman carry him.

LUCE
But hear me.

ISABELLA

I am in love sweet Luce, and you are so skilfull, that I must needs undo my self; and hear me, let Oliver pack up my Glass discreetly, and see my Curles well carried. O sweet Luce, you have a tongue, and open tongues have open you know what, Luce.

LUCE
Pray you be satisfied.

ISABELLA
Yes and contented too, before I leave you: there's a Roger, which some call a Butcher, I speak of certainties, I do not fish Luce, nay do not stare, I have a tongue can talk too: and a Green Chamber Luce, a back door opens to a long Gallerie; there was a night Luce, do you perceive, do you perceive me yet? O do you blush Luce? a Friday night I saw your Saint, Luce: for t'other box of Marmalade, all's thine sweet Roger, this I heard and kept too.

LUCE
E'ne as you are a woman Mistress.

ISABELLA
This I allow as good and Physical sometime, these meetings, and for the cheering of the heart; but Luce, to have your own turn served, and to your friend to be a dog-bolt.

LUCE
I confess it Mistress.

ISABELLA
As you have made my sister jealous of me, and foolishly, and childishly pursued it, I have found out your haunt, and traced your purposes; for which mine honour suffers; your best waies must be applied to bring her back again, and seriously and suddenly, that so I may have a means to clear my self, and she a fair opinion of me, else you peevish—

LUCE
My power and prayers Mistress.

ISABELLA
What's the matter?

[Enter **SHORTHOSE** and **WIDOW**.

SHORTHOSE
I have been with the Gentleman, he has it, much good may do him with it.

WIDOW
Come, are you ready? you love so to delay time, the day grows on.

ISABELLA
I have sent for a few trifles, when those are come; And now I know your reason.

WIDOW

Know your own honour then, about your business, see the Coach ready presently, I'le tell you more then.

[Exit **LUCE** and **SHORTHOSE**.

And understand it well, you must not think your sister so tender eyed as not to see your follies, alas I know your heart, and must imagine, and truly too; 'tis not your charitie can coin such sums to give away as you have done, in that you have no wisdom Isabel, no nor modesty, where nobler uses are at home; I tell you, I am ashamed to find this in your years, far more in your discretion, none to chuse but things for pity, none to seal your thoughts on, but one of no abiding, of no name; nothing to bring you to but this, cold and hunger: A jolly Joynture sister, you are happy, no mony, no not ten shillings.

ISABELLA
You search nearly.

WIDOW
I know it as I know your folly, one that knows not where he shall eat his next meal, take his rest, unless it be i'th' stocks; what kindred has he, but a more wanting Brother, or what vertues.

ISABELLA
You have had rare intelligence, I see, sister.

WIDOW
Or say the man had vertue, is vertue in this age a full inheritance? what Joynture can he make you, Plutarchs Morals, or so much penny rent in the small Poets? this is not well, 'tis weak, and I grieve to know it.

ISABELLA
And this you quit the town for?

WIDOW
Is't not time?

ISABELLA
You are better read in my affairs than I am, that's all I have to answer, I'le go with you, and willingly, and what you think most dangerous, I'le sit laugh at. For sister 'tis not folly but good discretion governs our main fortunes.

WIDOW
I am glad to hear you say so.

ISABELLA
I am for you.

[Enter **SHORTHOSE**, and **HUMPHREY**, with riding rods.

HUMPHREY
The Devil cannot stay her, she'l on't, eat an egg now, and then we must away.

SHORTHOSE

I am gaul'd already, yet I will pray, may London wayes from henceforth be full of holes, and Coaches crack their wheels, may zealous Smiths so housel all our Hackneys, that they may feel compunction in their feet, and tire at High-gate, may it rain above all Almanacks till Carriers sail, and the Kings Fish-monger ride like Bike Arion upon a Trout to London.

HUMPHREY

At S. Albanes, let all the Inns be drunk, not an Host sober to bid her worship welcom.

SHORTHOSE

Not a Fiddle, but all preach't down with Puritans; no meat but Legs of Beef.

HUMPHREY

No beds but Wool-Packs.

SHORTHOSE

And those so crammed with Warrens of starved Fleas that bite like Bandogs; let Mims be angry at their S. Bel-Swagger, and we pass in the heat on't and be beaten, beaten abominably, beaten horse and man, and all my Ladies linnen sprinkled with suds and dish-water.

SHORTHOSE

Not a wheel but out of joynt.

[Enter **ROGER** laughing.

HUMPHREY

Why dost thou laugh?

ROGER

There's a Gentleman, and the rarest Gentleman, and makes the rarest sport.

SHORTHOSE

Where, where?

ROGER

Within here, h'as made the gayest sport with Tom the Coachman, so tewed him up with Sack that he lies lashing a But of Malmsie for his Mares.

SHORTHOSE

'Tis very good.

ROGER

And talks and laughs, and sings the rarest songs, and Shorthose, he has so maul'd the Red Deer pies, made such an alms i'th' butterie.

SHORTHOSE

Better still.

[Enter **VALENTINE**, **WIDOW**.

HUMPHREY
My Lady in a rage with the Gentleman?

SHORTHOSE
May he anger her into a feather.

[Exeunt.

WIDOW
I pray tell me, who sent you hither? for I imagine it is not your condition, you look so temperately, and like a Gentleman, to ask me these milde questions.

VALENTINE
Do you think I use to walk of errands, gentle Lady, or deal with women out of dreams from others?

WIDOW
You have not known me sure?

VALENTINE
Not much.

WIDOW
What reason have you then to be so tender of my credit, you are no kinsman?

VALENTINE
If you take it so, the honest office that I came to do you, is not so heavy but I can return it: now I perceive you are too proud, not worth my visit.

WIDOW
Pray stay, a little proud.

VALENTINE
Monstrous proud, I griev'd to hear a woman of your value, and your abundant parts stung by the people, but now I see 'tis true, you look upon me as if I were a rude and saucie fellow that borrowed all my breeding from a dunghil, or such a one, as should now fall and worship you in hope of pardon: you are cozen'd Lady, I came to prove opinion a loud liar, to see a woman only great in goodness, and Mistress of a greater fame than fortune, but—

WIDOW
You are a strange Gentleman, if I were proud now, I should be monstrous angry, which I am not, and shew the effects of pride; I should despise you, but you are welcom Sir: To think well of our selves, if we deserve it, it is a lustre in us, and every good we have, strives to shew gracious, what use is it else? old age like Seer-trees, is seldom seen affected, stirs sometimes at rehearsal of such acts as his daring youth endeavour'd.

VALENTINE

This is well, and now you speak to the purpose, you please me, but to be place proud?

WIDOW

If it be our own, why are we set here with distinction else, degrees, and orders given us? In you men, 'tis held a coolness, if you lose your right, affronts and loss of honour: streets, and walls, and upper ends of tables, had they tongues could tell what blood has followed, and what feud about your ranks; are we so much below you, that till you have us, are the tops of nature, to be accounted drones without a difference? you will make us beasts indeed.

VALENTINE

Nay worse than this too, proud of your cloaths, they swear a Mercers Lucifer, a tumour tackt together by a Taylour, nay yet worse, proud of red and white, a varnish that butter-milk can better.

WIDOW

Lord, how little will vex these poor blind people! if my cloaths be sometimes gay and glorious, does it follow, my mind must be my Mercers too? or say my beauty please some weak eyes, must it please them to think, that blows me up, that every hour blows off? this is an Infants anger.

VALENTINE

Thus they say too, what though you have a Coach lined through with velvet, and four fair Flanders mares, why should the streets be troubled continually with you, till Carmen curse you? can there be ought in this but pride of shew Lady, and pride of bum-beating, till the learned lawyers with their fat bags, are thrust against the bulks till all their causes crack? why should this Lady, and t'other Lady, and the third sweet Lady, and Madam at Mile-end, be daily visited, and your poorer neighbours, with course napfes neglected, fashions conferr'd about, pouncings, and paintings, and young mens bodies read on like Anatomies.

WIDOW

You are very credulous, and somewhat desperate, to deliver this Sir, to her you know not, but you shall confess me, and find I will not start; in us all meetings lie open to these lewd reports, and our thoughts at Church, our very meditations some will swear, which all should fear to judge, at least uncharitably, are mingled with your memories, cannot sleep, but this sweet Gentleman swims in our fancies, that scarlet man of war, and that smooth senior; not dress our heads without new ambushes, how to surprize that greatness, or that glorie; our very smiles are subject to constructions; nay Sir, it's come to this we cannot pish, but 'tis a favour for some fool or other: should we examine you thus, wer't not possible to take you without Perspectives?

VALENTINE

It may be, but these excuse not.

WIDOW

Nor yours force no truth Sir, what deadly tongues you have, and to those tongues what hearts, and what inventions? O' my conscience, and 'twere not for sharp justice, you would venture to aim at your own mothers, and account it glorie to say you had done so: all you think are counsels, and cannot erre, 'tis we still that shew double, giddy, or gorg'd with passion; we that build Babels for mens conclusions, we that scatter, as day does his warm light; our killing curses over Gods creatures, next to the devils malice: lets intreat your good words.

VALENTINE

Well, this woman has a brave soul.

WIDOW

Are not we gaily blest then, and much beholding to you for your substance? you may do what you list, we what beseems us, and narrowly do that too, and precisely, our names are served in else at Ordinaries, and belcht abroad in Taverns.

VALENTINE

O most brave Wench, and able to redeem an age of women.

WIDOW

You are no Whoremasters? Alas, no, Gentlemen, it were an impudence to think you vicious: you are so holy, handsome Ladies fright you, you are the cool things of the time, the temperance, meer Emblems of the Law, and veils of Vertue, you are not daily mending like Dutch Watches, and plastering like old Walls; they are not Gentlemen, that with their secret sins increase our Surgeons, and lie in Foraign Countries, for new sores; Women are all these Vices; you are not envious, false, covetous, vain-glorious, irreligious, drunken, revengeful, giddie-eyed like Parrots, eaters of others honours.

VALENTINE

You are angry.

WIDOW

No by my troth, and yet I could say more too, for when men make me angry, I am miserable.

VALENTINE

Sure 'tis a man, she could not bear it thus bravely else, it may be I am tedious.

WIDOW

Not at all, Sir, I am content at this time you should trouble me.

VALENTINE

You are distrustful.

WIDOW

Where I find no truth, Sir.

VALENTINE

Come, come, you are full of passion.

WIDOW

Some I have, I were too near the nature o' God else.

VALENTINE

You are monstrous peevish.

WIDOW

Because they are monstrous foolish, and know not how to use that should try me.

VALENTINE
I was never answered thus; were you never drunk Lady?

WIDOW
No sure, not drunk, Sir; yet I love good Wine, as I love health and joy of heart, but temperately, why do you ask that question?

VALENTINE
For that sin that they most charge you with, is this sin's servant, they say you are monstrous—

WIDOW
What, Sir, what?

VALENTINE
Most strangely.

WIDOW
It has a name sure?

VALENTINE
Infinitely lustful, without all bounds, they swear you kill'd your Husband.

WIDOW
Let us have it all for Heavens sake, 'tis good mirth, Sir.

VALENTINE
They say you will have four now, and those four stuck in four quarters, like four winds to cool you: will she not cry nor curse?

WIDOW
On with your story.

VALENTINE
And that you are forcing out of dispensations with sums of money to that purpose.

WIDOW
Four Husbands! should not I be blest, Sir, for example? Lord, what should I do with them? turn a Malt-mill, or Tithe them out like Town-bulls to my Tenants, you come to make me angry, but you cannot.

VALENTINE
I'le make you merry then, you are a brave Woman, and in despite of envy a right one, go thy wayes, truth thou art as good a Woman, as any Lord of them all can lay his Leg over, I do not often commend your Sex.

WIDOW
It seems so, your commendations are so studied for.

VALENTINE
I came to see you and sift you into Flowr to know your pureness, and I have found you excellent, I thank you; continue so, and shew men how to tread, and women how to follow: get an Husband, an honest man, you are a good woman, and live hedg'd in from scandal, let him be too an understanding man, and to that stedfast; 'tis pity your fair Figure should miscarry, and then you are fixt: farewel.

WIDOW
Pray stay a little, I love your company now you are so pleasant, and to my disposition set so even.

VALENTINE
I can no longer.

[Exit.

WIDOW
As I live a fine fellow, this manly handsome bluntness shews him honest; what is he, or from whence? bless me, four Husbands! how prettily he fooled me into Vices, to stir my jealousie, and find my nature; a proper Gentleman: I am not well o'th' sudden, such a companion I could live and dye with, his angers are meer mirth.

[Enter **ISABELLA**.

ISABELLA
Come, come, I am ready.

WIDOW
Are you so?

ISABELLA
What ails she? the Coach stales, and the people, the day goes on, I am as ready now as you desire, Sister: fie, who stays now, why do you sit and pout thus?

WIDOW
Prethee be quiet, I am not well.

ISABELLA
For Heav'us sake let's not ride staggering in the night, come, pray you take some Sweet-meats in your pocket, if your stomach—

WIDOW
I have a little business.

ISABELLA
To abuse me, you shall not find new dreams, and new suspicions, to horse withal.

WIDOW
Lord who made you a Commander! hey ho, my heart.

ISABELLA

Is the wind come thither, and Coward like, do you lose your Colours to 'em? are you sick o'th' Valentine? sweet Sister, come let's away, the Country will so quicken you, and we shall live so sweetly: Luce, my Ladies Cloak; nay, you have put me into such a gog of going, I would not stay for all the world; if I live here, you have so knock'd this love into my head, that I shall love any body, and I find my body, I know not how, so apt—pray let's be gone, Sister, I stand on thorns.

WIDOW

I prethee Isabella, i'faith I have some business that concerns me, I will suspect no more, here, wear that for me, and I'le pay the hundred pound you owe your Taylor.

[Enter **SHORTHOSE, ROGER, HUMPHREY, RALPH.**

ISABELLA

I had rather go, but—

WIDOW

Come walk in with me, we'll go to Cards, unsaddle the
Horses.

SHORTHOSE

A Jubile, a Jubile, we stay, Boys.

[Enter **UNCLE, LANCE, FOUNTAIN, BELLAMORE, HAIRBRAIN** following.

UNCLE

Are they behind us?

LANCE

Close, close, speak aloud, Sir.

UNCLE

I am glad my Nephew has so much discretion, at length to find his wants: did she entertain him?

LANCE

Most bravely, nobly, and gave him such a welcome!

UNCLE

For his own sake do you think?

LANCE

Most certain, Sir, and in his own cause bestir'd himself too, and wan such liking from her, she dotes on him, h'as the command of all the house already.

UNCLE

He deals not well with his friends.

LANCE
Let him deal on, and be his own friend, he has most need of her.

UNCLE
I wonder they would put him—

LANCE
You are in the right on't, a man that must raise himself, I knew he would couzen 'em, and glad I am he has: he watched occasion, and found it i'th' nick.

UNCLE
He has deceived me.

LANCE
I told you howsoever he wheel'd about, he would charge home at length: how I could laugh now, to think of these tame fools!

UNCLE
'Twas not well done, because they trusted him, yet.

BELLAMORE
Hark you Gentlemen.

UNCLE
We are upon a business, pray excuse us, they have it home.

LANCE
Come let it work good on Gentlemen.

[Exeunt **UNCLE, LANCE.**

FOUNTAIN
'Tis true, he is a knave, I ever thought it.

HAIRBRAIN
And we are fools, tame fools.

BELLAMORE
Come let's go seek him, he shall be hang'd before he colt us basely.

[Exeunt.

[Enter **ISABELLA, LUCE.**

ISABELLA
Art sure she loves him?

LUCE

Am I sure I live? and I have clapt on such a commendation on your revenge.

ISABELLA
Faith, he is a pretty Gentleman.

LUCE
Handsome enough, and that her eye has found out.

ISABELLA
He talks the best they say, and yet the maddest.

LUCE
H'as the right way.

ISABELLA
How is she?

LUCE
Bears it well, as if she cared not, but a man may see with half an eye through all her forced behaviour, and find who is her Valentine.

ISABELLA
Come let's go see her, I long to prosecute.

LUCE
By no means Mistress, let her take better hold first.

ISABELLA
I could burst now.

[Exeunt.

[Enter **VALENTINE, FOUNTAIN, BELLAMORE, HAIRBRAIN.**

VALENTINE
Upbraid me with your benefits, you Pilchers, you shotten, sold, slight fellows? was't not I that undertook you first from empty barrels, and brought those barking mouths that gaped like bung-holes to utter sence? where got you understanding? who taught you manners and apt carriage to rank your selves? who filled you in fit Taverns? were those born with your worships when you came hither? what brought you from the Universities of moment matter to allow you, besides your small base sentences?

BELLAMORE
'Tis well, Sir.

VALENTINE
Long Cloaks with two-hand-rapiers, boot-hoses with penny-poses, and twenty fools opinions, who looked on you but piping rites that knew you would be prizing, and Prentices in Paul's Church-yard, that scented your want of Britains Books.

[Enter **WIDOW, LUCE, HAIRBRAIN.**

FOUNTAIN
This cannot save you.

VALENTINE
Taunt my integrity you Whelps?

BELLAMORE
You may talk the stock we gave you out, but see no further.

HAIRBRAIN
You tempt our patience, we have found you out, and what your trust comes to, ye're well feathered, thank us, and think now of an honest course, 'tis time; men now begin to look, and narrowly into your tumbling tricks, they are stale.

WIDOW
Is not that he?

LUCE
'Tis he.

WIDOW
Be still and mark him.

VALENTINE
How miserable will these poor wretches be when I forsake 'em! but things have their necessities, I am sorry, to what a vomit must they turn again, now to their own dear Dunghil breeding; never hope after I cast you off, you men of Motley, you most undone things below pity, any that has a soul and six-pence dares relieve you, my name shall bar that blessing, there's your Cloak, Sir, keep it close to you, it may yet preserve you a fortnight longer from the fool; your Hat, pray be covered, and there's the Sattin that your Worship sent me, will serve you at a Sizes yet.

FOUNTAIN
Nay, faith Sir, you may e'ne rub these out now.

VALENTINE
No such relique, nor the least rag of such a sordid weakness shall keep me warm, these Breeches are mine own, purchased, and paid for, without your compassion, a Christian Breeches founded in Black-Friers, and so I'le maintain 'em.

HAIRBRAIN
So they seem, Sir.

VALENTINE

Only the thirteen shillings in these Breeches, and the odd groat, I take it, shall be yours, Sir, a mark to know a Knave by, pray preserve it, do not displease more, but take it presently, now help me off with my Boots.

HAIRBRAIN
We are no Grooms, Sir.

VALENTINE
For once you shall be, do it willingly, or by this hand I'le make you.

BELLAMORE
To our own, Sir, we may apply our hands.

VALENTINE
There's your Hangers, you may deserve a strong pair, and a girdle will hold you without buckles; now I am perfect, and now the proudest of your worships tell me I am beholding to you.

FOUNTAIN
No such matter.

VALENTINE
And take heed how you pity me, 'tis dangerous, exceeding dangerous, to prate of pity; which are the poorer? you are now puppies; I without you, or you without my knowledge? be Rogues, and so be gone, be Rogues and reply not, for if you do—

BELLAMORE
Only thus much, and then we'll leave you: the Air is far sharper than our anger, Sir, and these you may reserve to rail in warmer.

HAIRBRAIN
Pray have a care, Sir, of your health.

[Exit **LOVERS**.

VALENTINE
Yes Hog-hounds, more than you can have of your wits; 'tis cold, and I am very sensible, extreamly cold too, yet I will not off, till I have shamed these Rascals; I have indured as ill heats as another, and every way if one could perish my body, you'll bear the blame on't; I am colder here, not a poor penny left.

[Enter **UNCLE** with a Bag.

UNCLE
'Thas taken rarely, and now he's flead he will be ruled.

LANCE
To him, tew him, abuse him, and nip him close.

UNCLE

Why how now, Cousin, sunning your self this weather?

VALENTINE

As you see, Sir, in a hot fit, I thank my friends.

UNCLE

But Cousin, where are your Cloaths man? those are no inheritance, your scruple may compound with those I take it, this is no fashion, Cousin.

VALENTINE

Not much followed, I must confess; yet Uncle I determine to try what may be done next Term.

LANCE

How came you thus, Sir, for you are strangely moved.

VALENTINE

Rags, toys and trifles, fit only for those fools that first possessed 'em, and to those Knaves they are rendred. Freemen, Uncle, ought to appear like innocents, old Adam, a fair Fig-leaf sufficient.

UNCLE

Take me with you, were these your friends, that clear'd you thus?

VALENTINE

Hang friends, and even reckonings that make friends.

UNCLE

I thought till now, there had been no such living, no such purchase, for all the rest is labour, as a list of honourable friends; do such men as you, Sir, in lieu of all your understandings, travels, and those great gifts of nature, aim at no more than casting off your Coats? I am strangely cozen'd.

LANCE

Should not the Town shake at the cold you feel now, and all the Gentry suffer interdiction, no more sense spoken, all things Goth and Vandal, till you be summed again, Velvets and Scarlets, anointed with gold Lace, and Cloth of silver turned into Spanish Cottens for a penance, wits blasted with your Bulls and Taverns withered, as though the Term lay at St. Albans?

VALENTINE

Gentlemen, you have spoken long and level, I beseech you take breath a while and hear me; you imagine now, by the twirling of your strings, that I am at the last, as also that my friends are flown like Swallows after Summer.

UNCLE

Yes, Sir.

VALENTINE

And that I have no more in this poor Pannier, to raise me up again above your rents, Uncle.

UNCLE

All this I do believe.

VALENTINE
You have no mind to better me.

UNCLE
Yes, Cousin, and to that end I come, and once more offer you all that my power is master of.

VALENTINE
A match then, lay me down fifty pounds there.

UNCLE
There it is, Sir.

VALENTINE
And on it write, that you are pleased to give this, as due unto my merit, without caution of land redeeming, tedious thanks, or thrift hereafter to be hoped for.

UNCLE
How?

[**LUCE** lays a Suit and Letter at the door.

VALENTINE
Without daring, when you are drunk, to relish of revilings, to which you are prone in Sack, Uncle.

UNCLE
I thank you, Sir.

LANCE
Come, come away, let the young wanton play a while, away I say, Sir, let him go forward with his naked fashion, he will seek you too morrow; goodly weather, sultry hot, sultry, how I sweat!

UNCLE
Farewel, Sir.

[Exeunt **UNCLE** and **LANCE**.

VALENTINE
Would I sweat too, I am monstrous vext, and cold too; and these are but thin pumps to walk the streets in; clothes I must get, this fashion will not fadge with me; besides, 'tis an ill winter wear,—What art thou? yes, they are clothes, and rich ones, some fool has left 'em: and if I should utter—what's this paper here? Let these be only worn by the most noble and deserving Gentleman Valentine,—dropt out o'th' clouds! I think they are full of gold too; well, I'le leave my wonder, and be warm again, in the next house I'le shift.

[Exit.

ACTUS QUARTUS

SCÆNA PRIMA

Enter **FRANCISCO**, **UNCLE** and **LANCE**.

FRANCISCO
Why do you deal thus with him? 'tis unnobly.

UNCLE
Peace Cousin peace, you are too tender of him, he must be dealt thus with, he must be cured thus, the violence of his disease Francisco, must not be jested with, 'tis grown infectious, and now strong Corrosives must cure him.

LANCE
H'as had a stinger, has eaten off his clothes, the next his skin comes.

UNCLE
And let it search him to the bones, 'tis better, 'twill make him feel it.

LANCE
Where be his noble friends now? will his fantastical opinions cloath him, or the learned Art of having nothing feed him?

UNCLE
It must needs greedily, for all his friends have flung him off, he is naked, and where to skin himself again, if I know, or can devise how he should get himself lodging, his Spirit must be bowed, and now we have him, have him at that we hoped for.

LANCE
Next time we meet him cracking of nuts, with half a cloak about him, for all means are cut off, or borrowing sixpence, to shew his bounty in the pottage Ordinary?

FRANCISCO
Which way went he?

LANCE
Pox, why should you ask after him, you have been trimm'd already, let him take his fortune, he spun it out himself, Sir, there's no pitie.

UNCLE
Besides some good to you now, from this miserie.

FRANCISCO
I rise upon his ruines! fie, fie, Uncle, fie honest Lance.
Those Gentlemen were base people, that could so soon take fire to his destruction.

UNCLE
You are a fool, you are a fool, a young man.

[Enter **VALENTINE**.

VALENTINE
Morrow Uncle, morrow Frank, sweet Frank, and how, and how d'ee, think now, how shew matters? morrow Bandog.

UNCLE
How?

FRANCISCO
Is this man naked, forsaken of his friends?

VALENTINE
Th'art handsom, Frank, a pretty Gentleman, i'faith thou lookest well, and yet here may be those that look as handsom.

LANCE
Sure he can conjure, and has the Devil for his Tailor.

UNCLE
New and rich! 'tis most impossible he should recover.

LANCE
Give him this luck, and fling him into the Sea.

UNCLE
'Tis not he, imagination cannot work this miracle.

VALENTINE
Yes, yes, 'tis he, I will assure you Uncle, the very he, the he your wisdom plaid withall, I thank you for't, neighed at his nakednesse, and made his cold and poverty your pastime; you see I live, and the best can do no more Uncle, and though I have no state, I keep the streets still, and take my pleasure in the Town, like a poor Gentleman, wear clothes to keep me warm, poor things they serve me, can make a shew too if I list, yes uncle, and ring a peal in my pockets, ding dong, uncle, these are mad foolish wayes, but who can help 'em?

UNCLE
I am amazed.

LANCE
I'le sell my Copyhold, for since there are such excellent new nothings, why should I labour? is there no Fairy haunts him, no Rat, nor no old woman?

UNCLE

You are Valentine.

VALENTINE
I think so, I cannot tell, I have been call'd so, and some say Christened, why do you wonder at me, and swell, as if you had met a Sergeant fasting, did you ever know desert want? y'are fools, a little stoop there may be to allay him, he would grow too rank else, a small eclipse to shadow him, but out he must break, glowingly again, and with a great lustre, look you uncle, motion and majesty.

UNCLE
I am confounded.

FRANCISCO
I am of his faith.

VALENTINE
Walk by his careless kinsman, and turn again and walk, and look thus Uncle, taking some one by the hand, he loves best, leave them to the mercy of the hog-market, come Frank, Fortune is now my friend, let me instruct thee.

FRANCISCO
Good morrow Uncle, I must needs go with him.

VALENTINE
Flay me, and turn me out where none inhabits, within two hours I shall be thus again, now wonder on, and laugh at your own ignorance.

[Exit **VALENTINE** and **FRANCISCO**.

UNCLE
I do believe him.

LANCE
So do I, and heartily upon my conscience, burie him stark naked, he would rise again, within two hours imbroidered: sow mustard-seeds, and they cannot come up so thick as his new sattens do, and clothes of silver, there's no striving.

UNCLE
Let him play a while then, and let's search out what hand:—

LANCE
I, there the game lies.

[Exeunt.

[Enter **FOUNTAIN**, **BELLAMORE**, and **HAIRBRAIN**.

FOUNTAIN

Come, let's speak for our selves, we have lodg'd him sure enough, his nakedness dare not peep out to cross us.

BELLAMORE
We can have no admittance.

HAIRBRAIN
Let's in boldly, and use our best arts, who she deigns to favour, we are all content.

FOUNTAIN
Much good may do her with him, no civil wars.

BELLAMORE
By no means, now do I wonder in what old tod Ivie he lies whistling for means, nor clothes he hath none, nor none will trust him, we have made that side sure, teach him a new wooing.

HAIRBRAIN
Say it is his Uncles spite.

FOUNTAIN
It is all one Gentlemen, 'thas rid us of a fair incumbrance, and makes us look about to our own fortunes. Who are these?

[Enter **ISABELLA** and **LUCE**.

ISABELLA
Not see this man yet! well, I shall be wiser: but Luce, didst ever know a woman melt so? she is finely hurt to hunt.

LUCE
Peace, the three Suitors.

ISABELLA
I could so titter now and laugh, I was lost Luce, and I must love, I know not what; O Cupid, what pretty gins thou hast to halter Woodcocks! and we must into the Country in all haste, Luce.

LUCE
For Heaven's sake, Mistris.

ISABELLA
Nay, I have done, I must laugh though; but Scholar, I shall teach you.

FOUNTAIN
'Tis her sister.

BELLAMORE
Save you Ladies.

ISABELLA
Fair met Gentlemen, you are visiting my sister, I assure my self.

HAIRBRAIN
We would fain bless our eyes.

ISABELLA
Behold and welcom, you would see her?

FOUNTAIN
'Tis our business.

ISABELLA
You shall see her, and you shall talk with her.

LUCE
She will not see 'em, nor spend a word.

ISABELLA
I'le make her fret a thousand, nay now I have found the scab, I will so scratch her.

LUCE
She cannot endure 'em.

ISABELLA
She loves 'em but too dearly, come follow me, I'le bring you toth' party Gentlemen, then make your own conditions.

LUCE
She is sick you know.

ISABELLA
I'le make her well, or kill her, and take no idle answer, you are fools then, nor stand off for her state, she'l scorn you all then, but urge her still, and though she fret, still follow her, a widow must be won so.

BELLAMORE
She speaks bravely.

ISABELLA
I would fain have a Brother in law, I love mens company, and if she call for dinner to avoid you, be sure you stay; follow her into her chamber, if she retire to Pray, pray with her, and boldly, like honest lovers.

LUCE
This will kill her.

FOUNTAIN
You have shewed us one way, do but lead the tother.

ISABELLA
I know you stand o'thorns, come I'le dispatch you.

LUCE
If you live after this.

ISABELLA
I have lost my aim.

[Enter **VALENTINE** and **FRANCISCO**.

FRANCISCO
Did you not see 'em since.

VALENTINE
No hang 'em, hang 'em.

FRANCISCO
Nor will you not be seen by 'em?

VALENTINE
Let 'em alone Frank, I'le make 'em their own justice, and a jerker.

FRANCISCO
Such base discourteous Dog-whelps.

VALENTINE
I shall dog 'em, and double dog 'em, ere I have done.

FRANCISCO
Will you go with me, for I would fain find out this piece of bountie, it was the Widows man, that I am certain of.

VALENTINE
To what end would you go?

FRANCISCO
To give thanks.

VALENTINE
Hang giving thanks, hast not thou parts deserve it? it includes a further will to be beholding, beggars can do no more at door, if you will go, there lies your way.

FRANCISCO
I hope you will go.

VALENTINE

No not in ceremony, and to a woman, with mine own Father, were he living Frank; I would toth' Court with Bears first, if it be that wench, I think it is, for t'other's wiser, I would not be so lookt upon, and laught at, so made a ladder for her wit, to climb upon, for 'tis the tartest tit in Christendom, I know her well Frank, and have buckled with her, so lickt, and stroaked, flear'd upon, and flouted, and shown to Chambermaids, like a strange beast, she had purchased with her penny.

FRANCISCO
You are a strange man, but do you think it was a woman?

VALENTINE
There's no doubt on't, who can be there to do it else? besides the manner of the circumstances.

FRANCISCO
Then such courtesies, who ever does 'em sir, saving your own wisdom, must be more lookt into, and better answered, than with deserving slights, or what we ought to have conferred upon us, men may starve else, means are not gotten now with crying out I am a gallant fellow, a good Souldier, a man of learning, or fit to be employed, immediate blessings cease like miracles, and we must grow by second means, I pray go with me, even as you love me Sir.

VALENTINE
I will come to thee, but Frank, I will not stay to hear your fopperies, dispatch those e're I come.

FRANCISCO
You will not fail me.

VALENTINE
Some two hours hence expect me.

FRANCISCO
I thank you, and will look for you.

[Exeunt.

[Enter **WIDOW**, **SHORTHOSE** and **ROGER**.

WIDOW
Who let in these puppies? you blind rascals, you drunken
Knaves several.

SHORTHOSE
Yes forsooth, I'le let 'em in presently,—Gentlemen.

WIDOW
Sprecious, you blown Pudding, bawling Rogue.

SHORTHOSE
I bawl as loud as I can, would you have me fetch 'em upon my back.

WIDOW
Get 'em out rascal, out with 'em, out, I sweat to have 'em near me.

SHORTHOSE
I should sweat more to carry 'em out.

ROGER
They are Gentlemen Madam.

SHORTHOSE
Shall we get 'em into th' butterie, and make'em drunk?

WIDOW
Do any thing, so I be eased.

[Enter **ISABELLA, FOUNTAIN, BELLAMORE, HAIRBRAIN**.

ISABELLA
Now to her Sir, fear nothing.

ROGER
Slip aside boy, I know she loves 'em, howsoever she carries it, and has invited 'em, my young Mistress told me so.

SHORTHOSE
Away to tables then.

[Exeunt.

ISABELLA
I shall burst with the sport on't.

FOUNTAIN
You are too curious Madam, too full of preparation, we expect it not.

BELLAMORE
Me thinks the house is handsom, every place decent, what need you be vext?

HAIRBRAIN
We are no strangers.

FOUNTAIN
What though we come e're you expected us, do not we know your entertainments Madam are free, and full at all times?

WIDOW
You are merry, Gentlemen.

BELLAMORE

We come to be merry Madam, and very merry, men love to laugh heartily, and now and then Lady a little of our old plea.

WIDOW

I am busie, and very busie too, will none deliver me.

HAIRBRAIN

There is a time for all, you may be busie, but when your friends come, you have as much power Madam.

WIDOW

This is a tedious torment.

FOUNTAIN

How hansomly this little piece of anger shews upon her! well Madam well, you know not how to grace your self.

BELLAMORE

Nay every thing she does breeds a new sweetness.

WIDOW

I must go up, I must go up, I have a business waits upon me, some wine for the Gentlemen.

HAIRBRAIN

Nay, we'l go with you, we never saw your chambers yet.

ISABELLA

Hold there boyes.

WIDOW

Say I go to my prayers?

FOUNTAIN

We'l pray with you, and help your meditations.

WIDOW

This is boysterous, or say I go to sleep, will you go to sleep with me?

BELLAMORE

So suddenly before meat will be dangerous, we know your dinner's ready Lady, you will not sleep.

WIDOW

Give me my Coach, I will take the air.

HAIRBRAIN

We'l wait on you, and then your meat after a quickened stomach.

WIDOW

Let it alone, and call my Steward to me, and bid him bring his reckonings into the Orchard, these unmannerly rude puppies—

[Exit **WIDOW**.

FOUNTAIN
We'l walk after you and view the pleasure of the place.

ISABELLA
Let her not rest, for if you give her breath, she'l scorn and flout you, seem how she will, this is the way to win her, be bold and prosper.

BELLAMORE
Nay if we do not tire her.—

[Exeunt.

ISABELLA
I'le teach you to worm me, good Lady sister, and peep into my privacies to suspect me, I'le torture you, with that you hate, most daintily, and when I have done that, laugh at that you love most.

[Enter **LUCE**.

LUCE
What have you done, she chafes and fumes outragiously, and still they persecute her.

ISABELLA
Long may they do so, I'le teach her to declaim against my pities, why is she not gone out o'th' town, but gives occasion for men to run mad after her?

LUCE
I shall be hanged.

ISABELLA
This in me had been high treason, three at a time, and private in her Orchard! I hope she'l cast her reckonings right now.

[Enter **WIDOW**.

WIDOW
Well, I shall find who brought 'em.

ISABELLA
Ha, ha, ha.

WIDOW
Why do you laugh sister? I fear me 'tis your trick, 'twas neatly done of you, and well becomes your pleasure.

ISABELLA
What have you done with 'em?

WIDOW
Lockt 'em i'th' Orchard, there I'le make 'em dance and caper too, before they get their liberty, unmannerly rude puppies.

ISABELLA
They are somewhat saucy, but yet I'le let 'em out, and once more sound 'em, why were they not beaten out?

WIDOW
I was about it, but because they came as suiters.

ISABELLA
Why did you not answer 'em?

WIDOW
They are so impudent they will receive none: More yet! How came these in?

[Enter **FRANCISCO** and **LANCE**.

LANCE
At the door, Madam.

ISABELLA
It is that face.

LUCE
This is the Gentleman.

WIDOW
She sent the money to?

LUCE
The same.

ISABELLA
Fie leave you, they have some business.

WIDOW
Nay, you shall stay, Sister, they are strangers both to me; how her face alters!

ISABELLA
I am sorry he comes now.

WIDOW

I am glad he is here now though. Who would you speak with,
Gentlemen?

LANCE
You Lady, or your fair Sister there, here's a Gentleman that has received a benefit.

WIDOW
From whom, Sir?

LANCE
From one of you, as he supposes, Madam, your man delivered it.

WIDOW
I pray go forward.

LANCE
And of so great a goodness, that he dares not, without the tender of his thanks and service, pass by the house.

WIDOW
Which is the Gentleman?

LANCE
This, Madam.

WIDOW
What's your name, Sir?

FRANCISCO
They that know me call me Francisco, Lady, one not so proud to scorn so timely a benefit, nor so wretched to hide a gratitude.

WIDOW
It is well bestowed then.

FRANCISCO
Your fair self, or your Sister as it seems, for what desert I dare not know, unless a handsome subject for your charities, or aptness in your noble will to do it, have showred upon my wants a timely bounty, which makes me rich in thanks, my best inheritance.

WIDOW
I am sorry 'twas not mine, this is the Gentlewoman, fie, do not blush, go roundly to the matter, the man is a pretty man.

ISABELLA
You have three fine ones.

FRANCISCO

Then to you, dear Lady?

ISABELLA
I pray no more, Sir, if I may perswade you, your only aptness to do this is recompence, and more than I expected.

FRANCISCO
But good Lady.

ISABELLA
And for me further to be acquainted with it besides the imputation of vain glory, were greedy thankings of my self, I did it not to be more affected to; I did it, and if it happened where I thought it fitted, I have my end; more to enquire is curious in either of us, more than that suspicious.

FRANCISCO
But gentle Lady, 'twill be necessary.

ISABELLA
About the right way nothing, do not fright it, being to pious use and tender sighted, with the blown face of Complements, it blasts it; had you not come at all, but thought thanks, it had been too much, 'twas not to see your person.

WIDOW
A brave dissembling Rogue, and how she carries it!

ISABELLA
Though I believe few handsomer; or hear you, though I affect a good tongue well; or try you, though my years desire a friend, that I relieved you.

WIDOW
A plaguie cunning quean.

ISABELLA
For so I carried it, my end's too glorious in mine eyes, and bettered the goodness I propounded with opinion.

WIDOW
Fear her not, Sir.

ISABELLA
You cannot catch me, Sister.

FRANCISCO
Will you both teach, and tie my tongue up Lady?

ISABELLA
Let it suffice you have it, it was never mine, whilest good men wanted it.

LANCE
This is a Saint sure.

ISABELLA
And if you be not such a one, restore it.

FRANCISCO
To commend my self, were more officious than you think my thanks are, to doubt I may be worth your gift a treason, both to mine own good and understanding, I know my mind clear, and though modesty tells me, he that intreats intrudes; yet I must think something, and of some season, met with your better taste, this had not been else.

WIDOW
What ward for that, wench?

ISABELLA
Alas, it never touched me.

FRANCISCO
Well, gentle Lady, yours is the first money I ever took upon a forced ill manners.

ISABELLA
The last of me, if ever you use other.

FRANCISCO
How may I do, and your way to be thought a grateful taker?

ISABELLA
Spend it, and say nothing, your modesty may deserve more.

WIDOW
O Sister will you bar thankfulness?

ISABELLA
Dogs dance for meat, would ye have men do worse? for they can speak, cry out like Wood-mongers, good deeds by the hundreds, I did it that my best friend should not know it, wine and vain glory does as much as I else, if you will force my merit, against my meaning, use it in well bestowing it, in shewing it came to be a benefit, and was so; and not examining a Woman did it, or to what end, in not believing sometimes your self, when drink and stirring conversation may ripen strange perswasions.

FRANCISCO
Gentle Lady, I were a base receiver of a courtesie, and you a worse disposer, were my nature unfurnished of these fore-sights. Ladies honours were ever in my thoughts, unspotted Crimes, their good deeds holy Temples, where the incense burns not; to common eyes your fears are vertuous, and so I shall preserve 'em.

ISABELLA
Keep but this way, and from this place to tell me so, you have paid me; and so I wish you see all fortune.

[Exit.

WIDOW
Fear not, the Woman will be thanked, I do not doubt it. Are you so crafty, carry it so precisely? this is to wake my fears, or to abuse me, I shall look narrowly: despair not Gentlemen, there is an hour to catch a Woman in, if you be wise, so, I must leave you too; Now will I go laugh at my Suitors.

[Exit.

LANCE
Sir, what courage?

FRANCISCO
This Woman is a founder, and cites Statutes to all her benefits.

LANCE
I never knew yet, so few years and so cunning, yet believe me she has an itch, but how to make her confess it, for it is a crafty Tit, and plays about you, will not bite home, she would fain, but she dares not; carry your self but so discreetly, Sir, that want or wantonness seem not to search you, and you shall see her open.

FRANCISCO
I do love her, and were I rich, would give two thousand pound to wed her wit but one hour, oh 'tis a Dragon, and such a spritely way of pleasure, ha Lance.

LANCE
Your ha Lance broken once, you would cry, ho, ho, Lance.

FRANCISCO
Some leaden landed Rogue will have this wench now, when all's done, some such youth will carry her, and wear her, greasie out like stuff, some Dunce that knows no more but Markets, and admires nothing but a long charge at Sizes: O the fortunes!

[Enter **ISABELLA** and **LUCE**.

LANCE
Comfort your self.

LUCE
They are here yet, and alone too, boldly upon't; nay, Mistress, I still told you, how 'twould find your trust, this 'tis to venture your charity upon a boy.

LANCE
Now, what's the matter? stand fast, and like your self.

ISABELLA
Prethee no more Wench.

LUCE
What was his want to you?

ISABELLA
'Tis true.

LUCE
Or misery, or say he had been i'th' Cage, was there no mercy to look abroad but yours?

ISABELLA
I am paid for fooling.

LUCE
Must every slight companion that can purchase a shew of poverty and beggerly planet fall under your compassion?

LANCE
Here's a new matter.

LUCE
Nay, you are served but too well, here he staies yet, yet as I live.

FRANCISCO
How her face alters on me!

LUCE
Out of a confidence I hope.

ISABELLA
I am glad on't.

FRANCISCO
How do you gentle Lady?

ISABELLA
Much ashamed Sir, (but first stand further off me, y'are infectious) to find such vanitie, nay almost impudence, where I believ'd a worth: is this your thanks, the gratitude you were so mad to make me, your trim counsel Gentlemen?

LANCE
What, Lady?

ISABELLA
Take your device again, it will not serve Sir, the woman will not bite, you are finely cozened, drop it no more for shame.

LUCE

Do you think you are here Sir amongst your wast-coateers, your base wenches that scratch at such occasions? you are deluded: This is a Gentlewoman of a noble house, born to a better fame than you can build her, and eyes above your pitch.

FRANCISCO
I do acknowledge—

ISABELLA
Then I beseech you Sir, what could 'see, (speak boldly, and speak truly, shame the Devil,) in my behaviour of such easiness that you durst venture to do this?

FRANCISCO
You amaze me, this Ring is none of mine, nor did I drop it.

LUCE
I saw you drop it, Sir.

ISABELLA
I took it up too, still looking when your modesty should miss it, why, what a childish part was this?

FRANCISCO
I vow.

ISABELLA
Vow me no vowes, he that dares do this, has bred himself to boldness, to forswear too; there take your gew-gaw, you are too much pampered, and I repent my part, as you grow older grow wiser if you can, and so farewel Sir.

[Exeunt **ISABELLA** and **LUCE**.

LANCE
Grow wiser if you can? she has put it to you, 'tis a rich
Ring, did you drop it?

FRANCISCO
Never, ne're saw it afore, Lance.

LANCE
Thereby hangs a tail then: what slight she makes to catch her self! look up Sir, you cannot lose her if you would, how daintily she flies upon the Lure, and cunningly she makes her stops! whistle and she'l come to you.

FRANCISCO
I would I were so happy.

LANCE
Maids are Clocks, the greatest Wheel they show, goes slowest to us, and make's hang on tedious hopes; the lesser, which are concealed, being often oyl'd with wishes, flee like desires, and never leave that

motion, till the tongue strikes; she is flesh, blood and marrow, young as her purpose, and soft as pity; no Monument to worship, but a mould to make men in, a neat one, and I know how e're she appears now, which is near enough, you are stark blind if you hit not soon at night; she would venture forty pounds more but to feel a Flea in your shape bite her: drop no more Rings forsooth, this was the prettiest thing to know her heart by.

FRANCISCO
Thou putst me in much comfort.

LANCE
Put your self in good comfort, if she do not point you out the way, drop no more Rings, she'l drop her self into you.

FRANCISCO
I wonder my Brother comes not.

LANCE
Let him alone, and feed your self on your own fortunes; come be frolick, and let's be monstrous wise and full of counsel, drop no more Rings.

[Exeunt.

[Enter **WIDOW, FOUNTAIN, BELLAMORE, HAIRBRAIN.**

WIDOW
If you will needs be foolish you must be used so: who sent for you? who entertained you Gentlemen? who bid you welcom hither? you came crowding, and impudently bold; press on my patience, as if I kept a house for all Companions, and of all sorts: will 'have your wills, will vex me and force my liking from you I ne're ow'd you?

FOUNTAIN
For all this we will dine with you.

BELLAMORE
And for all this will have a better answer from you.

WIDOW
You shall never, neither have an answer nor dinner, unless you use me with a more staid respect, and stay your time too.

[Enter **ISABELLA, SHORTHOSE, ROGER, HUMPHREY, RALPH,** with dishes of meat.

ISABELLA
Forward with the meat now.

ROGER
Come Gentlemen, march fairly.

SHORTHOSE

Roger, you are a weak Serving-man, your white broath runs from you; fie, how I sweat under this Pile of Beef; an Elephant can do more! Oh for such a back now, and in these times, what might a man arrive at! Goose, grase you up, and Woodcock march behinde thee, I am almost foundred.

WIDOW

Who bid you bring the meat yet? away you knaves, I will not dine these two hours: how am I vext and chafed! go carry it back and tell the Cook, he's an arrant Rascal, to send before I called.

SHORTHOSE

Face about Gentlemen, beat a mournfull march then, and give some supporters, or else I perish—

[Exeunt **SERVANTS**.

ISABELLA

It does me much good to see her chafe thus.

HAIRBRAIN

We can stay Madam, and will stay and dwell here, 'tis good Air.

FOUNTAIN

I know you have beds enough, and meat you never want.

WIDOW

You want a little.

BELLAMORE

We dare to pretend no. Since you are churlish, we'l give you
Physick, you must purge this anger, it burns you and decays you.

WIDOW

If I had you out once, I would be at the charge of a portcullis for you.

[Enter **VALENTINE**.

VALENTINE

Good morrow noble Lady.

WIDOW

Good morrow Sir. How sweetly now he looks, and how full manly! what slaves were these to use him so!

VALENTINE

I come to look a young man I call Brother.

WIDOW

Such a one was here Sir, as I remember your own Brother, but gone almost an hour agoe.

VALENTINE

Good ee'n then.

WIDOW
You must not so soon Sir, here be some Gentlemen, it may be you are acquainted with 'em.

HAIRBRAIN
Will nothing make him miserable?

FOUNTAIN
How glorious!

BELLAMORE
It is the very he, does it rain fortunes, or has he a familiar?

HAIRBRAIN
How doggedly he looks too?

FOUNTAIN
I am beyond my faith, pray let's be going.

VALENTINE
Where are these Gentlemen?

WIDOW
Here.

VALENTINE
Yes I know 'em, and will be more familiar.

BELLAMORE
Morrow Madam.

WIDOW
Nay stay and dine.

VALENTINE
You shall stay till I talk with you, and not dine neither, but fastingly my fury, you think you have undone me, think so still, and swallow that belief, till you be company for Court-hand Clarks, and starved Atturnies, till you break in at playes like Prentices for three a groat, and crack Nuts with the Scholars in peny Rooms again, and fight for Apples, till you return to what I found you, people betrai'd into the hands of Fencers, Challengers, Tooth-drawers Bills, and tedious Proclamations in Meal-markets, with throngings to see Cutpurses: stir not, but hear, and mark, I'le cut your throats else, till Water works, and rumours of New Rivers rid you again and run you into questions who built Thames, till you run mad for Lotteries, and stand there with your Tables to glean the golden Sentences, and cite 'em secretly to Servingmen for sound Essayes, till Taverns allow you but a Towel room to Tipple Wine in, that the Bell hath gone for twice, and Glasses that look like broken promises, tied up with wicker protestations, English Tobacco with half Pipes, nor in half a year once burnt, and Bisket that Bawds have rubb'd their

gums upon like Corals to bring the mark again, tell these hour Rascals so, this most fatal hour will come again, think I sit down the looser.

WIDOW

Will you stay Gentlemen, a piece of Beef and a cold Capon, that's all, you know you are welcom.

HUMPHREY

That was cast to abuse us.

BELLAMORE

Steal off, the Devil is in his anger.

WIDOW

Nay I am sure you will not leave me so discourteously, now I have provided for you.

VALENTINE

What do you here? why do ye vex a woman of her goodness, her state and worth? can you bring a fair certificate that you deserve to be her footmen? husbands, you puppies? husbands for Whores and Bawds, away you wind suckers; do not look big, nor prate, nor stay, nor grumble and when you are gone, seem to laugh at my fury, and slight this Lady, I shall hear, and know this: and though I am not bound to fight for women, as far they are good I dare preserve 'em: be not too bold, for if you be, I'le swinge you monstrously without all pity, your honours now goe, avoid me mainly.

[Exeunt.

WIDOW

Well Sir, you have delivered me, I thank you, and with your nobleness prevented danger, their tongues might utter, we'll all go and eat Sir.

VALENTINE

No, no, I dare not trust my self with women, go to your meat, eat little, take less ease, and tie your body to a daily labour, you may live honestly, and so I thank you.

[Exit.

WIDOW

Well go thy ways, thou art a noble fellow, and some means I must work to have thee know it.

[Exit.

ACTUS QUINTUS

SCÆNA PRIMA

Enter **UNCLE** and **MERCHANT**.

UNCLE

Most certain 'tis her hands that hold him up, and her sister relieves Frank.

MERCHANT

I am glad to hear it: but wherefore do they not pursue this fortune to some fair end?

UNCLE

The women are too craftie, Valentine too coy, and Frank too bashfull, had any wise man hold of such a blessing, they would strike it out o'th' flint but they would form it.

[Enter **WIDOW** and **SHORTHOSE**.

MERCHANT

The Widow sure, why does she stir so early?

WIDOW

'Tis strange, I cannot force him to understand me, and make a benefit of what I would bring him: tell my sister I'le use my devotions at home this morning, she may if she please go to Church.

SHORTHOSE

Hey ho.

WIDOW

And do you wait upon her with a torch Sir.

SHORTHOSE

Hey ho.

WIDOW

You lazie Knave.

SHORTHOSE

Here is such a tinkle tanklings that we can ne're lie quiet, and sleep our prayers out. Ralph, pray emptie my right shooe that you made your Chamber-pot, and burn a little Rosemarie in't, I must wait upon my Lady. This morning Prayer has brought me into a consumption, I have nothing left but flesh and bones about me.

WIDOW

You drousie slave, nothing but sleep and swilling!

SHORTHOSE

Had you been bitten with Bandog fleas, as I have been, and haunted with the night Mare.

WIDOW

With an Ale-pot.

SHORTHOSE

You would have little list to morning Prayers, pray take my fellow Ralph, he has a Psalm Book, I am an ingrum man.

WIDOW
Get you ready quickly, and when she is ready wait upon her handsomely; no more, be gone.

SHORTHOSE
If I do snore my part out—

[Exit **SHORTHOSE**.

UNCLE
Now to our purposes.

MERCHANT
Good morrow, Madam.

WIDOW
Good morrow, Gentlemen.

UNCLE
Good joy and fortune.

WIDOW
These are good things, and worth my thanks, I thank you Sir.

MERCHANT
Much joy I hope you'l find, we came to gratulate your new knit marriage-band.

WIDOW
How?

UNCLE
He's a Gentleman, although he be my kinsman, my fair Niece.

WIDOW
Niece, Sir?

UNCLE
Yes Lady, now I may say so, 'tis no shame to you, I say a Gentleman, and winking at some light fancies, which you most happily may affect him for, as bravely carried, as nobly bred and managed.

WIDOW
What's all this? I understand you not, what Niece, what marriage-knot?

UNCLE
I'le tell plainly, you are my Niece, and Valentine the Gentleman has made you so by marriage.

WIDOW
Marriage?

UNCLE
Yes Lady, and 'twas a noble and vertuous part, to take a falling man to your protection, and buoy him up again to all his glories.

WIDOW
The men are mad.

MERCHANT
What though he wanted these outward things, that flie away like shadows, was not his mind a full one, and a brave one? You have wealth enough to give him gloss and outside, and he wit enough to give way to love a Lady.

UNCLE
I ever thought he would do well.

MERCHANT
Nay, I knew how ever he wheel'd about like a loose Cabine, he would charge home at length, like a brave Gentleman; Heavens blessing o' your heart Lady, we are so bound to honour you, in all your service so devoted to you.

UNCLE
Do not look so strange Widow, it must be known, better a general joy; no stirring here yet, come, come, you cannot hide 'em.

WIDOW
Pray be not impudent, these are the finest toyes, belike I am married then?

MERCHANT
You are in a miserable estate in the worlds account else, I would not for your wealth it come to doubting.

WIDOW
And I am great with child?

UNCLE
No, great they say not, but 'tis a full opinion you are with child, and great joy among the Gentlemen, your husband hath bestirred himself fairly.

MERCHANT
Alas, we know his private hours of entrance, how long, and when he stayed, could name the bed too, where he paid down his first-fruits.

WIDOW
I shall believe anon.

UNCLE

And we consider for some private reasons, you would have it private, yet take your own pleasure; and so good morrow, my best Niece, my sweetest.

WIDOW

No, no, pray stay.

UNCLE

I know you would be with him, love him, and love him well.

MERCHANT

You'l find him noble, this may beget—

UNCLE

It must needs work upon her.

[Exit **UNCLE** and **MERCHANT**.

WIDOW

These are fine bobs i'faith, married, and with child too! how long has this been, I trow? they seem grave fellows, they should not come to flout; married, and bedded, the world takes notice too! where lies this May-game? I could be vext extreamly now, and rail too, but 'tis to no end, though I itch a little, must I be scratcht I know not how, who waits there?

[Enter **HUMPHREY**, a **SERVANT**.

HUMPHREY

Madam.

WIDOW

Make ready my Coach quickly, and wait you only, and hark you Sir, be secret and speedy, inquire out where he lies.

HUMPHREY

I shall do it, Madam.

WIDOW

Married, and got with child in a dream! 'tis fine i'faith, sure he that did this, would do better waking.

[Exit.

[Enter **VALENTINE**, **FRANCISCO**, **LANCE**, and a **BOY** with a Torch.

VALENTINE

Hold thy Torch handsomely: how dost thou Frank? Peter Bassel, bear up.

FRANCISCO

You have fried me soundly, Sack do you call this drink?

VALENTINE
A shrewd dog, Frank, will bite abundantly.

LANCE
Now could I fight, and fight with thee.

VALENTINE
With me, thou man of Memphis?

LANCE
But that thou art mine own natural master, yet my sack says thou art no man, thou art a Pagan, and pawnest thy land, which a noble cause.

VALENTINE
No arms, nor arms, good Lancelot, dear Lance, no fighting here, we will have Lands boy, Livings, and Titles, thou shalt be a Vice-Roy, hang fighting, hang't 'tis out of fashion.

LANCE
I would fain labour you into your lands again, go to, it is behoveful.

FRANCISCO
Fie Lance, fie.

LANCE
I must beat some body, and why not my Master, before a stranger? charity and beating begins at home.

VALENTINE
Come, thou shalt beat me.

LANCE
I will not be compel'd, and you were two Masters, I scorn the motion.

VALENTINE
Wilt thou sleep?

LANCE
I scorn sleep.

VALENTINE
Wilt thou go eat?

LANCE
I scorn meat, I come for rompering, I come to wait upon my charge discreetly; for look you, if you will not take your Mortgage again, here do I lie S' George, and so forth.

VALENTINE
And here do I S' George, bestride the Dragon, thus with my Lance.

LANCE

I sting, I sting with my tail.

VALENTINE

Do you so, do you so, Sir? I shall tail you presently.

FRANCISCO

By no means, do not hurt him.

VALENTINE

Take this Nelson, and now rise, thou Maiden Knight of Malllgo, lace on thy Helmet of inchanted Sack, and charge again.

LANCE

I'le play no more, you abuse me, will you go?

FRANCISCO

I'le bid you good morrow, Brother, for sleep I cannot, I have a thousand fancies.

VALENTINE

Now thou art arrived, go bravely to the matter, and do something of worth, Frank.

LANCE

You shall hear from us.

[Exeunt **LANCE** and **FRANCISCO**.

VALENTINE

This Rogue, if he had been sober, sure had beaten me, is the most tettish Knave.

[Enter **UNCLE** and **MERCHANT**, **BOY** with a Torch.

UNCLE

'Tis he.

MERCHANT

Good morrow.

VALENTINE

Why, Sir, good morrow to you too, and you be so lusty.

UNCLE

You have made your Brother a fine man, we met him.

VALENTINE

I made him a fine Gentleman, he was a fool before, brought up amongst the midst of Small-Beer-Brew-houses, what would you have with me?

MERCHANT
I come to tell you, your latest hour is come.

VALENTINE
Are you my sentence?

MERCHANT
The sentence of your state.

VALENTINE
Let it be hang'd then, and let it be hang'd high enough, I may not see it.

UNCLE
A gracious resolution.

VALENTINE
What would you have else with me, will you go drink, and let the world slide, Uncle? Ha, ha, ha, boyes, drink Sack like Whey, boyes.

MERCHANT
Have you no feeling, Sir?

VALENTINE
Come hither Merchant: make me a supper, thou most reverent Land-catcher, a supper of forty pounds.

MERCHANT
What then, Sir?

VALENTINE
Then bring thy Wife along, and thy fair Sisters, thy Neighbours and their Wives, and all their trinkets, let me have forty Trumpets, and such Wine, we'll laugh at all the miseries of Mortgage, and then in state I'le render thee an answer.

MERCHANT
What say you to this?

UNCLE
I dare not say, nor think neither.

MERCHANT
Will you redeem your state, speak to the point, Sir?

VALENTINE
Not, not if it were mine heir in the Turks Gallies.

MERCHANT
Then I must take an order?

VALENTINE

Take a thousand, I will not keep it, nor thou shalt not have it, because thou camest i'th' nick, thou shalt not have it, go take possession, and be sure you hold it, hold fast with both hands, for there be those hounds uncoupled, will ring you such a knell, go down in glory, and march upon my land, and cry, All's mine; cry as the Devil did, and be the Devil, mark what an Echo follows, build fine March-panes, to entertain Sir Silk-worm and his Lady, and pull the Chappel down, and raise a Chamber for Mistress Silver-pin, to lay her belly in, mark what an Earthquake comes. Then foolish Merchant my Tenants are no Subjects, they obey nothing, and they are people too never Christened, they know no Law nor Conscience, they'll devour thee; and thou mortal, the stopple, they'll confound thee within three days; no bit nor memory of what thou wert, no not the Wart upon thy Nose there, shall be e're heard of more; go take possession, and bring thy Children down, to rost like Rabbets, they love young Toasts and Butter, Bow-bell Suckers; as they love mischief, and hate Law, they are Cannibals; bring down thy kindred too, that be not fruitful, there be those Mandrakes that will mollifie 'em, go take possession. I'le go to my Chamber, afore Boy go.

[Exeunt.

MERCHANT
He's mad sure.

UNCLE
He's half drunk sure: and yet I like this unwillingness to lose it, this looking back.

MERCHANT
Yes, if he did it handsomely, but he's so harsh and strange.

UNCLE
Believe it 'tis his drink, Sir, and I am glad his drink has thrust it out.

MERCHANT
Cannibals? if ever I come to view his Regiment, if fair terms may be had.

UNCLE
He tells you true, Sir, they are a bunch of the most boisterous Rascals disorder ever made, let 'em be mad once, the power of the whole Country cannot cool 'em, be patient but a while.

MERCHANT
As long as you will, Sir, before I buy a bargain of such
Runts, I'le buy a Colledge for Bears, and live among 'em.

[Enter **FRANCISCO**, **LANCE**, **BOY** with a Torch.

FRANCISCO
How dost thou now?

LANCE
Better than I was, and straighter, but my head's a Hogshead still, it rowls and tumbles.

FRANCISCO
Thou wert cruelly paid.

LANCE
I may live to requite it, put a Snaffle of Sack in my mouth and then ride me very well.

FRANCISCO
'Twas all but sport, I'le tell thee what I mean now, I mean to see this Wench.

LANCE
Where a Devil is she? and there were two, 'twere better.

FRANCISCO
Dost thou hear the Bell ring?

LANCE
Yes, yes.

FRANCISCO
Then she comes to prayers, early each morning thither: Now if I could but meet her, for I am of another mettle now.

[Enter **ISABELLA**, and **SHORTHOSE** with a Torch.

LANCE
What light's yon?

FRANCISCO
Ha, 'tis a light, take her by the hand and court her.

LANCE
Take her below the girdle, you'l never speed else, it comes on this way still, oh that I had but such an opportunity in a Saw-pit, how it comes on, comes on! 'tis here.

FRANCISCO
'Tis she: fortune I kiss thy hand—Good morrow Lady.

ISABELLA
What voice is that, Sirra, do you sleep as you go, 'tis he,
I am glad on't. Why, Shorthose?

SHORTHOSE
Yes forsooth, I was dreamt, I was going to Church.

LANCE
She sees you as plain as I do.

ISABELLA
Hold the torch up.

SHORTHOSE
Here's nothing but a stall, and a Butcher's Dog asleep in't, where did you see the voice?

FRANCISCO
She looks still angry.

LANCE
To her and meet Sir.

ISABELLA
Here, here.

FRANCISCO
Yes Lady, never bless your self, I am but a man, and like an honest man, now I will thank you—

ISABELLA
What do you mean, who sent for you, who desired you?

SHORTHOSE
Shall I put out the Torch forsooth?

ISABELLA
Can I not go about my private meditations, Ha, but such companions as you must ruffle me? you had best go with me Sir?

FRANCISCO
'Twas my purpose.

ISABELLA
Why, what an impudence is this! you had best, being so near the Church, provide a Priest, and perswade me to marry you.

FRANCISCO
It was my meaning, and such a husband, so loving, and so carefull, my youth, and all my fortunes shall arrive at—Hark you?

ISABELLA
'Tis strange you should be thus unmannerly, turn home again sirra, you had best now force my man to lead your way.

LANCE
Yes marry shall he Lady, forward my friend.

ISABELLA
This is a pretty Riot, it may grow to a rape.

FRANCISCO
Do you like that better? I can ravish you an hundred times, and never hurt you.

SHORTHOSE
I see nothing, I am asleep still, when you have done tell me, and then I'le wake Mistris.

ISABELLA
Are you in earnest Sir, do you long to be hang'd?

FRANCISCO
Yes by my troth Lady in these fair Tresses.

ISABELLA
Shall I call out for help?

FRANCISCO
No by no means, that were a weak trick Lady, I'le kiss, and stop your mouth.

ISABELLA
You'l answer all these?

FRANCISCO
A thousand kisses more.

ISABELLA
I was never abused thus, you had best give out too, that you found me willing, and say I doted on you?

FRANCISCO
That's known already, and no man living shall now carry you from me.

ISABELLA
This is fine i'faith.

FRANCISCO
It shall be ten times finer.

ISABELLA
Well, seeing you are so valiant, keep your way, I will to Church.

FRANCISCO
And I will wait upon you.

ISABELLA
And it is most likely there's a Priest, if you dare venture as you profess, I would wish you look about you, to do these rude tricks, for you know the recompences, and trust not to my mercy.

FRANCISCO

But I will Lady.

ISABELLA
For I'le so handle you.

FRANCISCO
That's it I look for.

LANCE
Afore thou dream.

SHORTHOSE
Have you done?

ISABELLA
Go on Sir, and follow if you dare.

FRANCISCO
If I do not, hang me.

LANCE
'Tis all thine own boy, an 'twere a million, god a mercy
Sack, when would small Beer have done this?

[Knocking within. Enter **VALENTINE**.

VALENTINE
Whose that that knocks and bounces, what a Devil ails you, is hell broke loose, or do you keep an Iron mill?

[Enter a **SERVANT**.

SERVANT
'Tis a Gentlewoman Sir that must needs speak with you.

VALENTINE
A Gentlewoman? what Gentlewoman, what have I to do with
Gentlewomen?

SERVANT
She will not be answered Sir.

VALENTINE
Fling up the bed and let her in, I'le try how gentle she is—

This Sack has fill'd my head so full of babies, I am almost mad; what Gentlewoman should this be? I hope she has brought me no butter print along with her to lay to my charge, if she have 'tis all one, I'le forswear it.

[Enter **WIDOW**.

WIDOW
O you're a noble Gallant, send off your Servant pray.

[Exit **SERVANT**.

VALENTINE
She will not ravish me? by this light she looks as sharp set as a Sparrow hawk, what wouldst thou woman?

WIDOW
O you have used me kindly, and like a Gentleman, this is to trust to you.

VALENTINE
Trust to me, for what?

WIDOW
Because I said in jest once, you were a handsom man, one I could like well, and fooling, made you believe I loved you, and might be brought to marrie.

VALENTINE
The widow is drunk too.

WIDOW
You out of this, which is a fine discretion, give out the matter's done, you have won and wed me, and that you have put, fairly put for an heir too, these are fine rumours to advance my credit: i'th' name of mischief what did you mean?

VALENTINE
That you loved me, and that you might be brought to marrie me? why, what a Devil do you mean, widow?

WIDOW
'Twas a fine trick too, to tell the world though you had enjoyed your first wish you wished, the wealth you aimed at, that I was poor, which is most true, I am, have sold my lands, because I love not those vexations, yet for mine honours sake, if you must be prating, and for my credits sake in the Town.

VALENTINE
I tell thee widow, I like thee ten times better, now thou hast no Lands, for now thy hopes and cares lye on thy husband, if e're thou marryest more.

WIDOW
Have not you married me, and for this main cause, now as you report it, to be your Nurse?

VALENTINE
My Nurse? why, what am I grown to, give me the Glass, my Nurse.

WIDOW

You n'er said truer, I must confess I did a little favour you, and with some labour might have been perswaded, but when I found I must be hourly troubled, with making broths, and dawbing your decayes with swadling, and with stitching up your ruines, for the world so reports.

VALENTINE

Do not provoke me.

WIDOW

And half an eye may see.

VALENTINE

Do not provoke me, the world's a lying world, and thou shalt find it, have a good heart, and take a strong faith to thee, and mark what follows, my Nurse, yes, you shall rock me: Widow I'le keep you waking.

WIDOW

You are disposed Sir.

VALENTINE

Yes marry am I Widow, and you shall feel it, nay and they touch my freehold, I am a Tiger.

WIDOW

I think so.

VALENTINE

Come.

WIDOW

Whither?

VALENTINE

Any whither.
[**Sings**.
The fit's upon me now, the fit's upon me now,
Come quickly gentle Ladie, the fit's upon me now,
The world shall know they're fools,
And so shalt thou do too,
Let the Cobler meddle with his tools,
The fit's upon me now.

Take me quickly, while I am in this vein, away with me, for if I have but two hours to consider, all the widows in the world cannot recover me.

WIDOW

If you will, go with me Sir.

VALENTINE
Yes marrie will I, but 'tis in anger yet, and I will marrie thee, do not cross me; yes, and I will lie with thee, and get a whole bundle of babies, and I will kiss thee, stand still and kiss me handsomely, but do not provoke me, stir neither hand nor foot, for I am dangerous, I drunk sack yesternight, do not allure me: Thou art no widow of this world, come in pitie, and in spite I'le marrie thee, not a word more, and I may be brought to love thee.

[Exeunt.

[Enter **MERCHANT**, and **UNCLE**, at several doors.

MERCHANT
Well met again, and what good news yet?

UNCLE
Faith nothing.

MERCHANT
No fruits of what we sowed?

UNCLE
Nothing I hear of.

MERCHANT
No turning in this tide yet?

UNCLE
'Tis all flood, and till that fall away, there's no expecting.

[Enter **FRANCISCO, ISABELLA, LANCE, SHORTHOSE**, a torch.

MERCHANT
Is not this his younger Brother?

UNCLE
With a Gentlewoman the widow's sister, as I live he smiles, he has got good hold, why well said Frank i'faith, let's stay and mark.

ISABELLA
Well, you are the prettiest youth, and so you have handled me, think you ha' me sure.

FRANCISCO
As sure as wedlock.

ISABELLA
You had best lie with me too.

FRANCISCO

Yes indeed will I, and get such black ey'd boyes.

UNCLE
God a Mercy, Frank.

ISABELLA
This is a merrie world, poor simple Gentlewomen that think no harm, cannot walk about their business, but they must be catcht up I know not how.

FRANCISCO
I'le tell you, and I'le instruct ye too, have I caught you, Mistress?

ISABELLA
Well, and it were not for pure pity, I would give you the slip yet, but being as it is.

FRANCISCO
It shall be better.

[Enter **VALENTINE**, **WIDOW**, and **RALPH**, with a torch.

ISABELLA
My sister, as I live, your Brother with her! sure, I think you are the Kings takers.

UNCLE
Now it works.

VALENTINE
Nay, you shall know I am a man.

WIDOW
I think so.

VALENTINE
And such proof you shall have.

WIDOW
I pray speak softly.

VALENTINE
I'le speak it out Widow, yes and you shall confess too, I am no Nurse-child, I went for a man, a good one, if you can beat me out o'th' pit.

WIDOW
I did but jest with you.

VALENTINE
I'le handle you in earnest, and so handle you: Nay, when my credit calls.

WIDOW
Are you mad?

VALENTINE
I am mad, I am mad.

FRANCISCO
Good morrow, Sir, I like your preparation.

VALENTINE
Thou hast been at it, Frank.

FRANCISCO
Yes faith, 'tis done Sir.

VALENTINE
Along with me then, never hang an arse, widow.

ISABELLA
'Tis to no purpose, sister.

VALENTINE
Well said Black-brows, advance your torches Gentlemen.

UNCLE
Yes, yes Sir.

VALENTINE
And keep your ranks.

MERCHANT
Lance, carrie this before him.

UNCLE
Carrie it in state.

[Enter **MUSICIANS, FOUNTAIN, HAIRBRAIN, BELLAMORE.**

VALENTINE
What are you, Musicians? I know your coming, and what are those behind you?

MUSICIANS
Gentlemen that sent us to give the Lady a good morrow.

VALENTINE
O I know them, come boy sing the song I taught you,
And sing it lustily, come forward Gentlemen, you're welcom,
Welcom, now we are all friends, go get the Priest ready,

And let him not be long, we have much business:
Come Frank, rejoyce with me, thou hast got the start boy,
But I'le so tumble after, come my friends lead,
Lead cheerfully, and let your Fiddles ring boyes,
My follies and my fancies have an end here,
Display the morgage Lance, Merchant I'le pay you,
And every thing shall be in joynt again.

UNCLE
Afore, afore.

VALENTINE
And now confess, and know, Wit without Money, sometimes gives the blow.

[Exeunt.

John Fletcher – A Short Biography

John Fletcher was born in December, 1579 in Rye, Sussex. He was baptised on December 20th.

As can be imagined details of much of his life and career have not survived and, accordingly, only a very brief indication of his life and works can be given.

His father, Richard Fletcher, was a successful and rather ambitious cleric. From being the Dean of Peterborough he moved on to become the Bishop of Bristol, Bishop of Worcester and finally, shortly before his death, the Bishop of London. He was also the chaplain to Queen Elizabeth.

When he was Dean of Peterborough, Richard Fletcher, witnessed the execution of Mary, Queen of Scots. It was said he "knelt down on the scaffold steps and started to pray out loud and at length, in a prolonged and rhetorical style, as though determined to force his way into the pages of history". He cried out at her death, "So perish all the Queen's enemies!" All very dramatic but the family did have strong links to the Arts.

Young Fletcher appears at the very young age of eleven to have entered Corpus Christi College at Cambridge University in 1591. There are no records that he ever took a degree but there is some small evidence that he was being prepared for a career in the church.

However what is clear is that this was soon abandoned as he joined the stream of people who would leave University and decamp to the more bohemian life of commercial theatre in London.

Unfortunately his father fell out with Queen Elizabeth but appears to have been on his way to rehabilitation before his death in 1596. At his death he was, however, mired in debt.

The upbringing of the now teenage Fletcher and his seven siblings now passed to his paternal uncle, the poet and minor official Giles Fletcher. Giles, who had the patronage of the Earl of Essex may have been a liability rather than an advantage to the young Fletcher. With Essex involved in the failed rebellion against Elizabeth Giles was also tainted by association.

By 1606 John Fletcher appears to have equipped himself with the talents to become a playwright. Initially this appears to have been for the Children of the Queen's Revels, then performing at the Blackfriars Theatre.

Commendatory verses by Richard Brome in the Beaumont and Fletcher 1647 folio place Fletcher in the company of Ben Jonson, although it is not known when this friendship began. Jonson, of course, was a leviathan of English Literature, so admired that many of his literary friends and colleagues were simply known as 'Sons of Ben'. Fletcher's frequent early collaborator, Francis Beaumont, was also a friend of Jonson's.

Fletcher's early career was marked by one significant failure; The Faithful Shepherdess, his adaptation of Giovanni Battista Guarini's Il Pastor Fido, which was performed by the Blackfriars Children in 1608. In the preface to the printed edition of his play, Fletcher explained the failure as due to his audience's faulty expectations. They expected a pastoral tragicomedy to feature dances, comedy, and murder, with the shepherds presented in conventional stereotypes – as Fletcher put it, wearing "gray cloaks, with curtailed dogs in strings." Fletcher's preface is however best known for its pithy definition of tragicomedy: "A tragicomedy is not so called in respect of mirth and killing, but in respect it wants [i.e., lacks] deaths, which is enough to make it no tragedy; yet brings some near it, which is enough to make it no comedy." A comedy, he went on to say, must be "a representation of familiar people." His preface is critical of drama that features characters whose action violates nature.

In that case, Fletcher appears to have been developing a new style faster than audiences could comprehend. By 1609, however, he had found his stride. With Beaumont, he wrote Philaster, which became a hit for the King's Men and began a profitable association between Fletcher and that company. Philaster appears also to have begun a trend for tragicomedy. Fletcher's influence has also been said to have inspired some features of Shakespeare's late romances, and certainly his influence on the tragicomic work of other playwrights is even more marked.

By the middle of the 1610s, Fletcher's plays had achieved a popularity that rivalled Shakespeare's and cemented the pre-eminence of the King's Men in Jacobean London. After Beaumont's retirement, necessitated by ill-health, and then his early death in 1616, Fletcher continued working, both singly and in collaboration, until his death in 1625. By that time, he had produced, or had been credited with, close to fifty plays. This body of work remained a major part of the King's Men's repertory until the closing of the theatres in 1642 due to the Civil War.

At the beginning of his career Fletcher's most important collaborator was Francis Beaumont. The two wrote together for close to a decade, first for the Children of the Queen's Revels, and then for the King's Men. According to an anecdote transmitted or invented by John Aubrey, they also lived together in Bankside, sharing clothes and having "one wench in the house between them." This domestic arrangement, if it existed, was ended by Beaumont's marriage in 1613, and their dramatic partnership ended after Beaumont fell ill, probably of a stroke, that same year.

At this point Fletcher had written many plays with Beaumont and several others on his own. He seems to have been regarded as quite a talent although it should be remembered that playwrights were required to be prolific, to easily work with other collaborators and to produce work of quality and commercial appeal very quickly.

The King's Men, run by Philip Henslowe, was the most prestigious of the theatre companies and Fletcher now had an increasingly close association with it.

Fletcher collaborated with Shakespeare on Henry VIII, The Two Noble Kinsmen, and the now lost Cardenio, which some scholars say was the basis for Lewis Theobald's play Double Falsehood. (Theobald is regarded as one of the best Shakespearean editors. Whether his play is based on Cardenio or on some other is not absolutely known although Theobald certainly promoted it as his revision of the lost Shakespeare/Fletcher play.)

A play that Fletcher also wrote by himself at this time, The Woman's Prize or the Tamer Tamed, is also regarded as a sequel to The Taming of the Shrew.

In 1616, with the death of Shakespeare, Fletcher now appears to have entered into an enhanced arrangement with the King's Men on very similar terms to Shakespeare's. Fletcher would now write exclusively for the King's Men until his own death almost a decade later.

As well as continuing his solo productions Fletcher was still collaborating with other playwrights, mainly Philip Massinger, who, in turn, would succeed him as the in-house playwright for the King's Men.

Fletcher's popularity continued throughout his life; indeed during the winter of 1621, he had three of his plays performed at court. His mastery is most notable in two dramatic types; tragicomedy and the comedy of manners.

John Fletcher died in 1625, it is thought of bubonic plague which, at the time, was undergoing further outbreaks.

He seems to have been buried in what is now Southwark Cathedral, although a precise location is not known. There is much made of an anecdote that Fletcher and Massinger (who died in 1640) share the same grave but it is more likely that both are buried within a few yards of each other and that the stone markers in the floor have confused the issue. One is marked 'Edmond Shakespeare 1607' and the other 'John Fletcher 1625' refers to Shakespeare's younger brother and the playwright. The churchyards were, more often than not, completely over-crowded and breeding grounds for disease. Precise record keeping was not a practiced skill.

During the later Commonwealth, many of the playwright's best-known scenes were kept alive as drolls. These were brief performances, usually condensed into one or two scenes and with the addition of music or song to satisfy the taste for plays while the theatres were closed under the Puritans. At the re-opening of the theatres in 1660, the plays in the Fletcher canon, in original form or revised, were by far the most common productions on the English stage. The most frequently revived plays suggest the developing taste for comedies of manners. Among the tragedies, The Maid's Tragedy and, especially, Rollo Duke of Normandy held the stage. Four tragicomedies (A King and No King, The Humorous Lieutenant, Philaster, and The Island Princess) were popular, perhaps in part for their similarity to and foreshadowing of heroic drama. Four comedies (Rule a Wife And Have a Wife, The Chances, Beggars' Bush, and especially The Scornful Lady) were also stage mainstays.

Despite his popularity, and it appears he was held in higher regard than Shakespeare at this time, his works steadily lost ground to those of Shakespeare and to new productions from other playwrights.

Since then Fletcher has increasingly become a subject only for occasional revivals and for specialists. Fletcher and his collaborators have been the subject of important bibliographic and critical studies, but the plays have been revived only infrequently.

Due to the frequent collaborations between all manner of playwrights, and the revisions carried out in later years, having a settled list of authorship to any given set of plays can be problematic. The works of Fletcher and others of this period most definitely fall into this category. It is as well to take into account that during this period theatres were quite often closed either due to outbreaks of the plague or to the prevailing political and moral climate. Printers, anxious to provide materials that would sell, were not above changing a name or two to enhance sales.

Although Fletcher collaborated most often with Beaumont and Massinger, it is believed that Massinger revised many of the plays some time after their original production. Other collaborators including Nathan Field, William Shakespeare, William Rowley and others also can be seen distinctly in Fletchers' works. Many modern scholars point out that Fletcher had many particular mannerisms but other playwrights would also duplicate these at times so allocating exact contributions of anyone to a play is somewhat of a detective case in many instances. However from the original folio printings or licensing via the Master of the Revels (the statutory licensing authority to approve and censor plays as well a hand in publication and printing of theatrical materials) as well as contemporary notes a fairly precise bibliography of the works can be given with only a few plays lacking substantial authority and provenance.

John Fletcher – A Concise Bibliography

This bibliography gives the most likely date of writing together with when published, revised or licensed by the Master or the Revels (This position within the royal household was originally for royal festivities, ie revels, and later to oversee stage censorship, until this function was transferred to the Lord Chamberlain in 1624).

Solo Plays
The Faithful Shepherdess, pastoral (written 1608–9; printed 1609)
The Tragedy of Valentinian, tragedy (1610–14; 1647)
Monsieur Thomas, comedy (c. 1610–16; 1639)
The Woman's Prize, or The Tamer Tamed, comedy (c. 1611; 1647)
Bonduca, tragedy (1611–14; 1647)
The Chances, comedy (c. 1613–25; 1647)
Wit Without Money, comedy (c. 1614; 1639)
The Mad Lover, tragicomedy (acted 5 January 1617; 1647)
The Loyal Subject, tragicomedy (licensed 16 November 1618; revised 1633; 1647)
The Humorous Lieutenant, tragicomedy (c. 1619; 1647)
Women Pleased, tragicomedy (c. 1619–23; 1647)
The Island Princess, tragicomedy (c. 1620; 1647)
The Wild Goose Chase, comedy (c. 1621; 1652)

The Pilgrim, comedy (c. 1621; 1647)
A Wife for a Month, tragicomedy (licensed 27 May 1624; 1647)
Rule a Wife and Have a Wife, comedy (licensed 19 October 1624; 1640)

Collaborations

With Francis Beaumont

The Woman Hater, comedy (1606; 1607)
Cupid's Revenge, tragedy (c. 1607–12; 1615)
Philaster, or Love Lies a-Bleeding, tragicomedy (c. 1609; 1620)
The Maid's Tragedy, Tragedy (c. 1609; 1619)
A King and No King, tragicomedy (1611; 1619)
The Captain, comedy (c. 1609–12; 1647)
The Scornful Lady, comedy (c. 1613; 1616)
Love's Pilgrimage, tragicomedy (c. 1615–16; 1647)
The Noble Gentleman, comedy (c. 1613; licensed 3 February 1626; 1647)

With Francis Beaumont & Philip Massinger

Thierry & Theodoret, tragedy (c. 1607; 1621)
The Coxcomb, comedy (c. 1608–10; 1647)
Beggars' Bush, comedy (c. 1612–13; revised 1622; 1647)
Love's Cure, comedy (c. 1612–13; revised 1625; 1647)

With Philip Massinger

Sir John van Olden Barnavelt, tragedy (August 1619; MS)
The Little French Lawyer, comedy (c. 1619–23; 1647)
A Very Woman, tragicomedy (c. 1619–22; licensed 6 June 1634; 1655)
The Custom of the Country, comedy (c. 1619–23; 1647)
The Double Marriage, tragedy (c. 1619–23; 1647)
The False One, history (c. 1619–23; 1647)
The Prophetess, tragicomedy (licensed 14 May 1622; 1647)
The Sea Voyage, comedy (licensed 22 June 1622; 1647)
The Spanish Curate, comedy (licensed 24 October 1622; 1647)
The Lovers' Progress or The Wandering Lovers, tragicomedy (licensed 6 December 1623; rev 1634; 1647)
The Elder Brother, comedy (c. 1625; 1637)

With Philip Massinger & Nathan Field

The Honest Man's Fortune, tragicomedy (1613; 1647)
The Queen of Corinth, tragicomedy (c. 1616–18; 1647)
The Knight of Malta, tragicomedy (c. 1619; 1647)

With William Shakespeare

Henry VIII, history (c. 1613; 1623)
The Two Noble Kinsmen, tragicomedy (c. 1613; 1634)
Cardenio, tragicomedy (c. 1613)

With Thomas Middleton & William Rowley

Wit at Several Weapons, comedy (c. 1610–20; 1647)

The Maid in the Mill (licensed 29 August 1623; 1647).

Four Plays, or Moral Representations, in One, morality (c. 1608–13; 1647)

Rollo Duke of Normandy, or The Bloody Brother, tragedy (c. 1617; revised 1627–30; 1639)

The Night Walker, or The Little Thief, comedy (c. 1611; 1640)
The Coronation c. 1635

The Nice Valour, or The Passionate Madman, comedy (c. 1615–25; 1647)
The Laws of Candy, tragicomedy (c. 1619–23; 1647)
The Fair Maid of the Inn, comedy (licensed 22 January 1626; 1647)
The Faithful Friends, tragicomedy (registered 29 June 1660; MS.)

The Nice Valour is possibly by Fletcher revised by Thomas Middleton;

The Fair Maid of the Inn is perhaps a play by Massinger, John Ford, and John Webster, either with or without Fletcher's involvement.

The Laws of Candy has been variously attributed to Fletcher and to John Ford.

The Night-Walker was a Fletcher original, with additions by Shirley for a 1639 production.

Even now there is not absolute certainty on several of the plays. The first Beaumont & Fletcher folio of 1647 contained 35 plays and the second folio of 1679 added a further 18. In total 53 plays.

The first folio included The Masque of the Inner Temple and Gray's Inn (1613), and the second The Knight of the Burning Pestle (1607), widely considered Beaumont's solo works, although the latter was in early editions attributed to both writers. Fletcher himself said that Beaumont was attributed so-authorship of many works that belonged solely to Fletcher or to other collaborators.

One play in the canon, Sir John Van Olden Barnavelt, existed in manuscript and was not published till 1883.